Studying
SPIES

English
& Media
Centre

Acknowledgements

Credits

Written and edited by Barbara Bleiman and Lucy Webster

Cover: Rebecca Scambler

Printed by: Polestar Wheatons

Published by: The English and Media Centre, 18 Compton Terrace, London, N1 2UN

© English and Media Centre, 2005

ISBN: 0-907016-89-8

Acknowledgements

Guardian Newspapers Limited for 'The Digested Read'; Robert Opie for images from *The Wartime Scrapbook*; Penguin for the extract from *deadkidsongs* by Toby Litt; Faber and Faber for the extracts from *Spies* by Michael Frayn and *Five Boys* by Mick Jackson.

Thanks also to Michael Frayn for giving so generously of his time and to all the teachers who attended the course on 'Teaching *Spies*' at the English and Media Centre, April 2005.

Every effort has been made to trace and acknowledge copyright, but if accidental infringement has been made, we would welcome information to redress the situation.

A note on the text

Page references in the study guide refer to the paperback edition of *Spies* published by Faber and Faber in 2002.

Study Guide Contents

DVD Contents		4
Introduction		5
A Route Through		6
Before Reading		7
Reading the novel	Charting the narrative voice/time frames – ongoing	11
	Chapter 1	12
	Chapter 2	13
	Chapter 3	18
	Chapter 4	27
	Chapter 5	31
	Chapter 6	37
	Chapter 7	42
	Chapter 8	43
	Chapter 9	45
	Chapter 10	48
	Chapter 11	50
After Reading	An interview with Michael Frayn	54
	A response chain	56
	Spies – the title	56
	Book covers	56
	Male and female characters	58
	A novel about perception	59
	Growing up – a bildungsroman	59
	Narrative perspective	60
	Knowing and not knowing	65
	Structure	66
	Chronological and narrative time	69
	Openings and endings	70
	Instant revision	72
	The pace of the novel – a debate	73
	Life as a story	73
	Challenging oppositions	74
	Genre	75
	Two more novels for comparison	81
Critical Responses	The digested read	84
	The critics	84
	Writing a book club guide	90
Teachers' Notes		91

© English and Media Centre, 2005 — Studying *Spies*

DVD Contents

Section	Length of clip
An interview with Michael Frayn	
1. The idea of the book	
a) The germ of the story	1'47"
b) A spy story	0'48"
2. Childhood	
a) Children's views	0'42"
b) Children and power	1'00"
c) Rules and expectations	2'00"
d) Status and hierarchies	0'54"
3. Wartime England	3'19"
4. England and Germany	
a) The Second World War	1'25"
b) An interest in Germany	1'35"
c) Dislocation and identity	2'15"
5. Why 'Spies'?	1'29"
6. The theme of perception	1'52"
7. The female world	
a) Barbara and Mrs. Hayward	1'12"
b) The growth of sexuality	2'46"
8. The two narrators	2'20"
9. Motifs – the privet	1'40"
10. The process of writing	1'00"
11. Readers' responses	
a) German readers	0'55"
b) Writing for readers	0'43"
The complete interview with Michael Frayn	33'00"

A slideshow
1. Images from the 1940s
2. Book covers

Introduction

Studying Spies – an overview

Studying Spies is a flexible resource which provides support for reading, analysing and writing about the novel. It includes a wide range of activities on plot, theme and character including drama, role-play, charting, creative writing and visual representations. There is, however, a particular focus on some of the trickier aspects of the novel: narrative structure, perspective and voice. To gain confidence in writing about form, structure and language (AO3), Literature students are encouraged to explore the novel from a linguistic perspective in unusual and well-supported ways. Contextual material (historical, social and literary) and a diverse range of provocative critical extracts are integrated into the study of the novel in ways which develop students' critical and creative skills.

The study guide is complemented and extended by an EMC interview with Michael Frayn on DVD. Topics covered include: the process of writing; the world of the novel; the theme of spying; the methods of narration; the structure of the novel; representations of childhood; the use of motifs; the 1940s. The DVD also includes a slideshow of colour versions of the images reproduced in black and white in the study guide.

How the study guide is organised

The study guide is divided into four sections:
- Before Reading
- Reading the Novel
- After Reading
- Critical Responses

There is also a section of 'Teachers' Notes' providing brief guidance on some of the activities which might require more teacher input (for example mapping the locations, segmenting the novel and linguistic approaches to the text).

Using the study guide

While the material in 'Reading the Novel' focuses on key aspects of each chapter, it is structured as a route through the novel, providing students with opportunities to speculate about what will happen (e.g. predictive role-play, discussion, creative writing activities). If your students have read the novel on their own before coming to study it in class, you may want to pick out some of these prediction activities to support their independent reading.

Even if you are reading parts of the novel in class, you may want to hold back some of the longer activities on specific chapters in order that the reading of the novel itself is not interrupted for too long.

The guide includes far more activities than any class could cover in the time available; it is not intended that you work through all the material but that you select from it, depending on the needs of your students and what you feel to be particularly important aspects of the novel. One possible route through the material and the novel is offered on page 6.

Using the DVD

There is an extended activity using the interview with Michael Frayn in 'After Reading' (page 54). If students have read the novel on their own, the interview would be a good bridge between this first independent read and more focused, analytical study.

Suitable places for showing extracts from the interview are indicated in 'Reading the Novel' by the following icon: [DVD] with the number of the clip underneath.

A Route Through

Week	Class	Homework
0	Preparation for the first full week of reading.	'Childhood memories' (page 8).
1	'A few extracts from the novel' (page 7). Listen to some of the childhood memory pieces (page 8). 'Perception – a classroom experiment' (page 8). Share thoughts on the paradox and expectations of the novel. Read Chapter 1 out loud and do 'Group work on Chapter 1' (page 12). Set up 'Charting the narrative voice' (page 11).	'A paradox' (page 7) plus expectations of the novel. Read Chapter 2.
2	Feed back on Chapter 2 including 'The last line' (page 13). 'The narrative voice' (page 13); 'Keith and Stephen' (page 17) and 'Motifs' (page 18). 'A classroom experiment – one week later' (page 8). Feed back on Chapter 3; 'Annotating fragments' (page 24); 'Life in the Second World War' (page 18). Set up 'Becoming an expert' (page 27), allocating different aspects to each group.	Read Chapter 3 and 'The most important points' (page 24). Read Chapter 4 focusing on the aspect allocated for 'Becoming an expert' (page 27).
3	Group work on Chapter 4 followed by presentations to the class ('Becoming an expert' page 27). 'Narrative voice' (page 27; see also page 11). 'Map of the locations' (see pages 14 and 26). Feed back on 'A shift in perspective' (page 31). 'A close focus on style' (page 31) and 'Before reading on – the tunnel' (page 33).	Read Chapter 5 up to page 89 including 'A shift in perspective' (page 31). Read the rest of Chapter 5 and do 'What is the chapter about?' (page 34).
4	Feed back on 'What is the chapter about? Finding evidence' (page 34). Very brief, oral version of 'Writing the next section' (page 37). Read Chapter 6, stopping at the points listed in 'Predicting and titling' (page 37). 'Before reading the chapter' on page 42 and update 'Narrative voice' chart (page 11); 'Reading the Chapter' up to the end of page 141; 'Before reading pages 142 to the end' (page 42). Read the rest of the chapter and do 'All my betrayals and failures' (page 42).	'What does Stephen think now?' (pages 37-38). 'Summing up the Chapter' (page 42).
5	Feed back on 'Summing up the Chapter' (page 42). Read up to page 162 of the novel and do 'Barbara Berrill, Stephen and the reader' (page 43). Read the rest of the chapter and do 'Sequencing the events' (page 43). Set up 'A boxing match' (page 44) for students to prepare at home. 'A boxing match' (page 44); 'Secrets and betrayals' (page 44).	Prepare for 'A boxing match' (page 44). Read 1st section of Chapter 9 and script the dialogue for 'The conversation' (page 45).
6	Listen to a few examples of 'The conversation' (page 45). Read the rest of Chapter 9 in sections to page 181 'The basket – Stephen's dilemma' (page 45); to 187 'Barbara and the basket' (page 46); to 190 'Can I have a word with you old chap?'. Do the freeze-frame activity (page 46). 'Just a minute' debate (page 47); Work on the motifs: 'A value for x' (page 47). Read Chapter 10, then complete 'The game's finally over' (page 48); 'Hero or coward' (page 49); speculation about the man in the Barn using 'Stephen' (page 47) and 'Looking for clues' (page 48).	Prepare for 'Just a minute' (page 47). Predicting the ending using 'What now? Predictions' (page 50).
7	Listen to predictions. Read up to page 228 and do 'A revelation' (page 50). Read the rest of Chapter 11 and write a personal response using a combination of 'A personal response' (page 51), 'An appropriate ending' (page 51), 'Summing up the novel' (page 53) and 'A response chain' (page 56). Feed back on 'Back to the beginning' (page 52). 'An interview with Michael Frayn' (page 54).	'Back to the beginning' (page 52). 'Instant revision' – preparation (page 72).
8-12	'Instant revision' – presentation (page 72). 'Narrative perspective – First explorations' (page 60). 'Narrative perspective – The shifting perspective' (page 64). 'Narrative structure – Patterns, shifts and repetition' (page 67). 'Openings and endings' (page 70). 'Genre' (page 75) or 'Two more novels for comparison' (page 81). 'Critical responses – The digested read' (page 84). 'Critical responses – The critics' (page 84).	'Narrative structure – Segmenting the novel' (page 66). 'Male and female characters' (page 58).

Before Reading

A paradox

> Everything is as it was, I discover when I reach my destination, and everything has changed.

This phrase is taken from early in the novel and it recurs in different forms several times.

- Talk about the phrase and explore the paradox.
- What might it tell you about the novel you're going to read?

A few extracts from the novel

Below are four extracts from the novel.

- Talk about what impressions they give you of the kind of novel this is going to be.
- Go on to explore anything you find interesting about:
  – the narrative voice
  – the use of tenses
  – the balance of narration, events, dialogue and reflection.

> 1. I look up at the sky, the one feature of every landscape and townscape that endures from generation to generation and century to century. Even the sky has changed. Once the war was written across it in a tangled scribble of heroic vapour trails. There were the upraised fingers of the searchlights at night, and the immense coloured palaces of falling flares. Now even the sky has become mild and bland. (*Page 10*)

> 2. Everything that we'd once taken for granted now seems open to question. Even what appears to be happening directly in front of your eyes, you realise when you think about it, turns out to be something you can't actually quite see after all, to involve all kinds of assumptions and interpretations. (*Pages 41-42*)

> 3. The sound that's changed, I realise, is the sound of my breathing. It's grown more complex. It no longer corresponds precisely to the rise and fall I can feel inside my chest.
>
>   I stop breathing. The sound of breathing continues. (*Page 117*)

> 4. What he wanted, I think, was for all the shifting thoughts inside his head to cease, for everything to stop happening and to go back to what it had been before. The clean simplicity of espionage, that had promised so well, had turned into such a sticky mess. (*Page 141*)

© English and Media Centre, 2005 — Studying *Spies*

Before Reading

Perception – a classroom experiment

6   In interview Michael Frayn said:

> I think the philosophical seed of this story is the question of perception, how we make sense of what's in front of our eyes, how we see it through our own ideas and our own narratives.
>
> I think what the book is really about is how people make sense of the world in front of them. I mean if you think about the way we look at things, for a start it seems very obvious, you just look at the world, and the world comes into your head, and you see what's in front of your eyes, but the more you think about it, the more you realise it's not like that, that you have to interpret what's in front of your eyes in order to see it. You bring your own ideas to bear on it, and you see it through the stories you have heard about it, the stories you have told about it yourself. This is true of everyone, adults as well as children, but it's perhaps more visible in the case of children because they see the world in a subtly different way.

- In the last ten minutes of your lesson, write a description of what happened during the lesson. You can include anything that strikes you – not just the facts of what happened but also your thoughts, sensations and memories of important moments. Don't talk to anyone else about what you have written.

- Read out some of these accounts. What was similar or different about the way different people in the class perceived the lesson?

- Your teacher will collect in your writing.

A classroom experiment – one week later

- Without looking at what you originally wrote, write again about that same lesson. Feel free to put it in the context of what's happened in between if you want to, or focus most on what you now think it is important to say.

- Now listen to both the first and second accounts of one or two people. What has changed from one account to the next?

- As a group, discuss what you've learned about how people see the world. Make a list of some key points raised by this activity.

Childhood memories

One of the things Michael Frayn's novel is about is the past and childhood memories. The novel starts with this first paragraph:

> The third week of June, and there it is again: the same almost embarrassingly familiar breath of sweetness that comes every year about this time. I catch it on the warm evening air as I walk past the well-ordered gardens in my quiet street, and for a moment I'm a child again and everything's before me – all the frightening, half-understood promise of life. (*Page 3*)

- Talk about this opening and what ideas it raises about memory.

- To help you think about how Frayn evokes a child's world, think back to your own early childhood and try to evoke it for yourself through memories. Use the chart on page 9 of this study guide to record your memories. Look at the example on page 10 for someone who is in their fifties, to get you thinking about the kinds of things you might include.

Studying *Spies* © English and Media Centre, 2005

Before Reading

	Age 1-5	Age 5-10	Age 10-15
A smell			
A food/taste			
An item of clothing			
A phrase			
A song			
A place			
An object			
A TV programme/film			
A moment			
Something that's gone			

Before Reading

An example, filled in by a 52-year-old.

	Aged 5	Aged 8	Aged 10
A smell	Talcum powder	Warm school milk	Hyacinths
A food/taste	Ice cream and jelly	Spangles	Fray Bentos pie
An item of clothing	Start-rite red shoes	An apron, made at Brownies	Mini-skirt
A phrase	'Short back and sides'	'Swinging sixties'	'With it'
A song	'Ring a ring a roses'	'Bill and Ben'	'My Boy Lollipop'
A place	The woods opposite my home	An old church hall	The lido, that's now a multiplex cinema
An object	A pair of pink ballet shoes	Ford popular car	With the Beatles LP
A TV programme/film	No TV set	The Lone Ranger	Ready, Steady, Go
A moment	A nightmare about drowning	Sitting under the tree at school listening to a story	Hearing about the death of President Kennedy
Something that's gone	Hair ribbons	London smog	Vyella school shirts

Writing about memories – experimenting with narrative voice

- Use the memories in your chart to write two or three paragraphs about being a particular age, using a different narrative voice for each one. You could choose from the following:
  - first person narrator looking back
  - first person narrator, from close-up, as if it's happening now
  - all-knowing, distant third person narrator
  - indirect free style, in which the third person narrator sometimes seems to see things from the point of view of one person.

- Talk about the different effects you achieved using each of the narrative voices.

- When reading the novel, bear in mind what you've discovered about the range of possible narrative techniques for writing about memory.

Reading the Novel

Charting the narrative voice/time frames – an ongoing activity

■ As you read the novel, record any shifts you notice in the narrative voice and time frame (such as flashbacks, jumps forward) on the chart below.

Chapter and page	Shifts in narrative voice	Shifts in time frame
1	Adult voice of old man (whole chapter)	Old man prompted to think about his childhood by the smell of a particular plant.
2	p11	
3		
4		
5		
6		
7		
8		
9		
10		
11		

Reading the Novel – Chapter 1

Chapter 1

Group work on Chapter 1

- Listen to this chapter being read aloud.

- In small groups, focus on one aspect of the chapter, then feed back your ideas to the whole class. Pool your expectations of the rest of the novel.

Group 1 – The narrator

Is this a first or third person narrative? Does the narrator seem to be a character in the story? What do we find out about the narrator? What kind of voice does he have? Does he speak in the same tense throughout? Is it a voice of certainty? Is he a reliable narrator, one whose viewpoint you feel you can trust? Is he an all-knowing narrator, who stands above the action? Does it vary at all?

Group 2 – Oppositions, contrasts, paradoxes, oxymorons

The chapter sets up all kinds of conflicting feelings. What are they? How does the writer use contrast, oppositions and oxymorons to create the narrator's disturbing, contradictory feelings?

(Note: an oxymoron is the putting together of two seemingly opposite things, for instance the phrase 'bittersweet' is an oxymoron.)

Group 3 – Questions

The first chapter is full of questions. What are these? Why are there so many? Are there any answers? What kind of effect does all this questioning have on the reader? What questions is the reader left with at the end of this chapter?

Group 4 – Drawing the reader in

Is this a good opening chapter for a novel? Does it draw the reader in and, if so, how? How does it go about introducing the characters and giving the reader a sense of what kind of novel this is going to be?

Group 5 – Themes

Are there any early indications in this first chapter of the kinds of themes that are going to be raised in the novel? What are they and how are they introduced?

Group 6 – Characters

Jot down all the names mentioned in this first chapter. What do you find out about them? How are they introduced? How can you tell whether they are going to be significant or not?

Reading the Novel – Chapter 2

Chapter 2

After reading the first page

In 'Before Reading' you read and talked about this phrase:

> Everything is as it was, I discover when I reach my destination, and everything has changed. (*Page 9*)

- Read up to the end of the sentence at the top of page 10 ('And yet after fifty years...') and talk about this paradox and what it now means to you.
- Now read Chapter 2.

After reading Chapter 2

The last line

- Talk about the effect of this chapter ending on you as a reader. Where do you think the book will go from here?

The narrative voice

In this chapter, there are important changes in the voice of the narrator and the point of view from which the story is told. These are summarised below.

- Old man first person narrator; uses present tense to tell the story of what he is doing now.
- Old man first person narrator re-constructing his memories of childhood; uses the third person to refer to his childhood self; shifts between past and present tense.
- Stephen as a child uses first person and present tense to tell the story of his childhood; includes more dialogue.

- Look back through the chapter to find examples of the three points of view and to identify where the shifts take place.

Some of the main features of the different narrative voices and points of view are included in the list above.

- Make a note of anything else you find interesting about the way the story is narrated in this chapter. (You might, for example, think about why the older narrator says on page 31 of the novel 'No, wait. I've got that wrong.' and later 'Or have I got everything back to front? Had the policeman already happened before this?')

- Share your observations and talk about the effect on both the story and the reader of Frayn's decision to use a shifting narrative voice and point of view.

- Use the chart on page 11 to continue tracking shifts in the narrative voice as you read.

You will be coming back to look at these shifts in more detail after reading the novel.

The place, then and now

The narrative moves between describing the place as it is now and as it was in the past, when the narrator was a child.

- Talk about your impressions of the Close and its inhabitants then.
- What, if anything, has changed? What has remained the same?

Reading the Novel – Chapter 2

A map of the locations

In this novel, locations are particularly important.

- Use the information in the story so far (for instance on pages 9 and 11 of the novel) to begin to make a large map of some of the key places. Do it in pencil to allow you to make changes and leave plenty of space to add to the map, as you read on. Later on, you will need to extend the map beyond the small area you know about now. Put all the information you can onto the map; for instance, if you're given the name of the family living in a particular house, put it on the house.

You could use the cut-outs below and on pages 15-16 if you find it helpful.

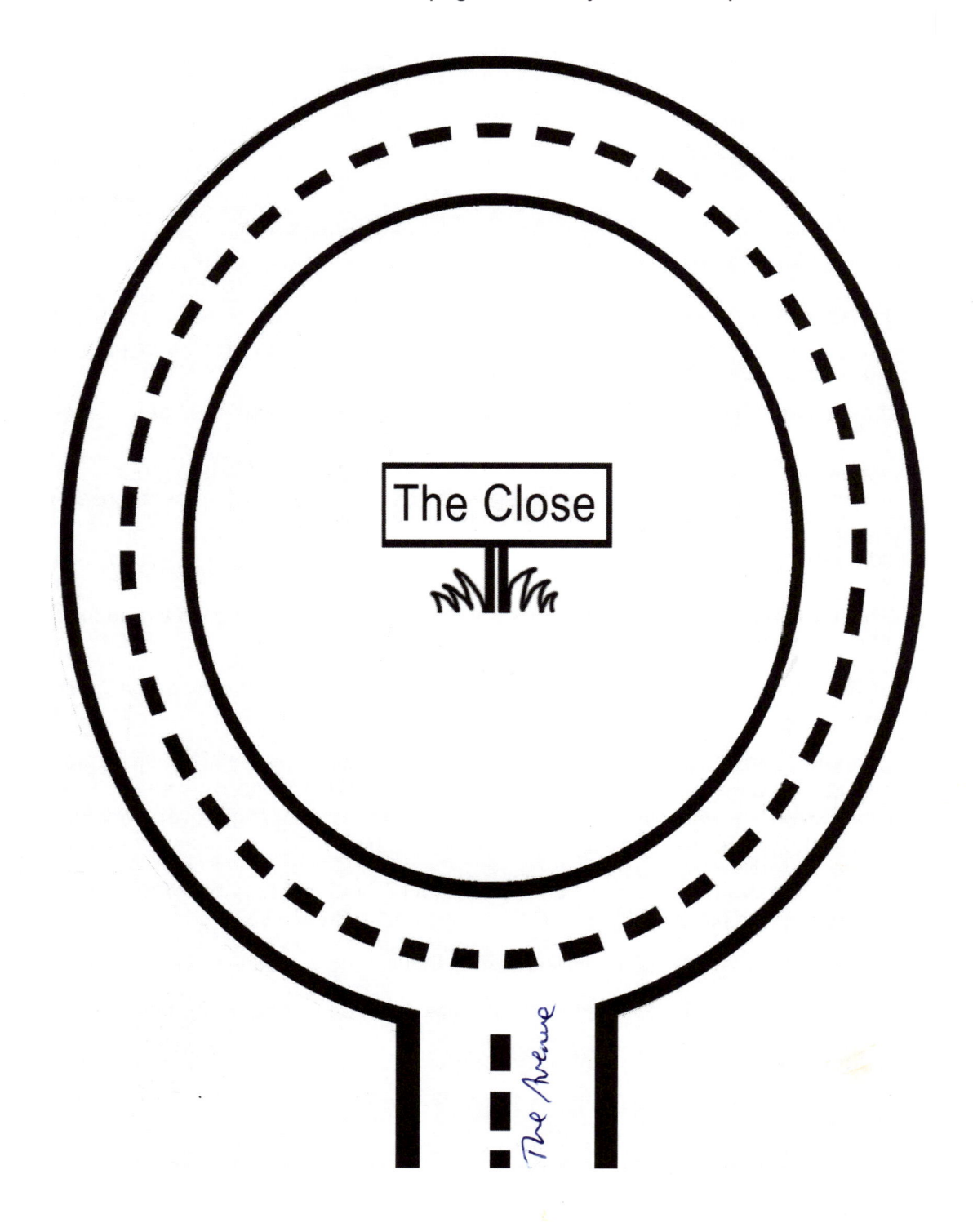

The Close

The Avenue

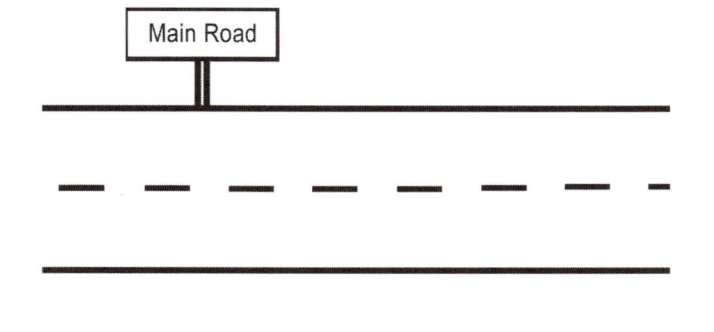

Reading the Novel – Chapter 2

Main Road

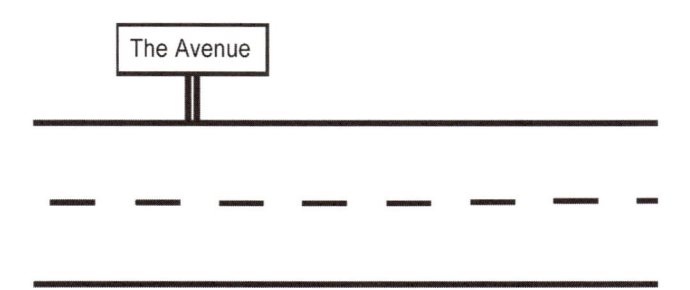

The Avenue

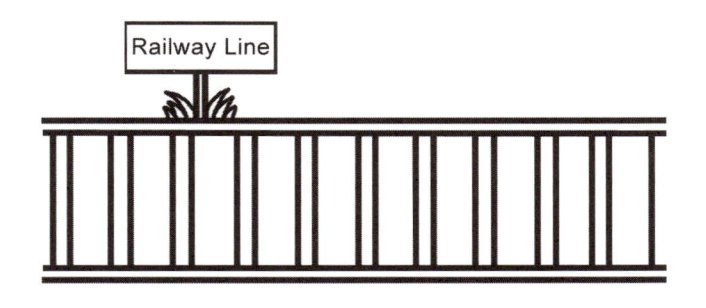

Railway Line

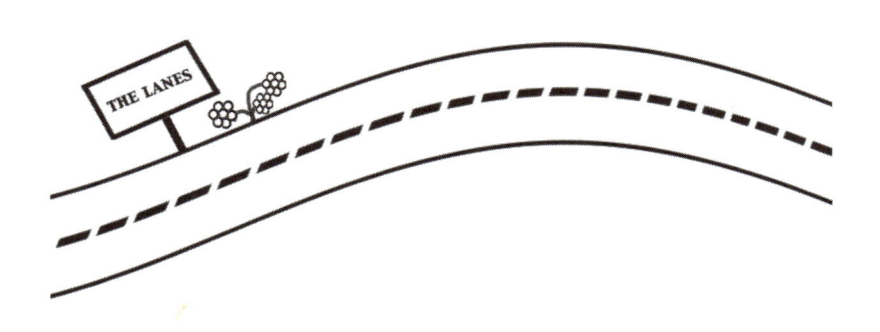

THE LANES

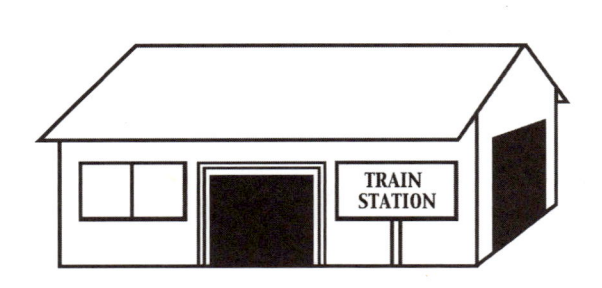

TRAIN STATION

Studying *Spies*

Reading the Novel – Chapter 2

Reading the Novel – Chapter 2

Keith and Stephen

In this chapter, we are given a great deal of information about Stephen and his friend Keith and lots of indications about the nature of their relationship.

- Look closely at how Michael Frayn rapidly paints a picture of the friendship through:
  - the houses (No 2, now called Wentworth, and No. 9 Chollerton)
  - the clothes worn
  - the parents
  - the playroom and the games played
  - social rituals
  - Stephen's own family and how they are viewed by him and the Haywards
  - the way the characters speak.

You could share these out between pairs and report back on what you have found out.

The characters

Some of the key characters in the story are introduced in this chapter: Stephen's mother, his father, Keith, Mrs. Hayward, Mr. Hayward, Auntie Dee and Uncle Peter.

- Put the names of the characters as headings on a sheet of A3 and make a list of between five and 10 adjectives to describe each of them, as they appear so far. If you use adjectives from the novel, put them in quotation marks, or put a short quotation next to your own adjective as evidence. One example has been given for you below:

> Mr Hayward
> 1. hard-working: 'Keith's father worked and worked'
> 2. 'impatient'
> 3. frightening

What do you know about Stephen?

- Pull together all your ideas about Stephen, both child and adult, drawn from this chapter. Write a fifty-word summary of his character.
- Compare summaries with other people in the class.
- Add to your own summary anything important that you've left out.

Unanswered questions

Despite the rich detail in the descriptions of characters and places, the author also withholds information from the reader, or introduces small details that seem important but are left unexplained. For instance, we are told that Keith's mother goes to Auntie Dee's house but Auntie Dee never goes to Keith's house. Why should this be? The narrator says when he did once see her there he knew something was wrong but we're not told what.

- Collect together all the instances you can find of half-information being given that makes you want to know more.
- Talk about why Frayn may offer us half-truths and gaps. Listed below are some ideas you might consider.
  - It creates suspense.
  - The child doesn't know or has forgotten, so these gaps will never be filled in.
  - Frayn is saying something about how perception works – there is no 'complete' story or single truth.

Reading the Novel – Chapter 3

Chapter 3

Before reading Chapter 3

Motifs

The following objects all play a particularly significant role in the story and in Stephen's perception of what is going on. These 'motif' words, each standing for a complex range of feelings, associations and values, are part of the structure of the novel.

- In pairs, brainstorm all the possible associations of these words or symbols, as a spidergram or mind map.
  - x
  - Photograph
  - Scarf
  - Bayonet
  - Privet
  - Slime
  - Germs

- Feed back your ideas about the possible significance the objects might have in the story, then create a class spidergram.

- Keep returning to your spidergram as you continue reading, adding to and amending your first ideas and finding short quotations to illustrate your thoughts. You should also add any other objects which you recognise as motifs.

Life in the Second World War

Slideshow 1 The images on pages 19-23 show posters, adverts, comic books, cigarette packets and so on from the Second World War. You can also see the images in colour on the DVD.

- Look at the images and talk about what impression you get of the following:
  - childhood
  - family life
  - the role of women
  - the role of men
  - homes, shops, food.

- Add in anything else you already know about the period.

3
- Watch Michael Frayn talking about growing up in the suburbs during the Second World War, then share your response to what he says. How does his description of a wartime childhood compare with your expectations?

- As you read Chapters 3 and 4, think about how the world depicted in *Spies* compares with the impression the images and interview have given you. After reading these chapters use small post-it notes to annotate the images with quotations from, and references to *Spies*.

Childhood

2a
2c
2d

- Watch the DVD clip of Michael Frayn talking about children and pull out what you consider to be the main points he makes. Share these as a class.

- As you read, look for the way the ideas and opinions revealed in his comments are explored in the rest of the novel.

Reading the Novel – Chapter 3

Studying *Spies*

Reading the Novel – Chapter 3

Reading the Novel – Chapter 3

Reading the Novel – Chapter 3

22 Studying *Spies* © English and Media Centre, 2005

Reading the Novel – Chapter 3

Reading the Novel – Chapter 3

During reading Chapter 3

The most important points

- Read Chapter 3 and make a list of what happens.

- When you have read the chapter, look back at your list, select what you think are the three most important points and then share your decisions as a whole class.

Filling in the gaps

- As you read, make a note at the point where gaps in the narrative leave you asking questions.

- After reading the chapter, try to answer your questions, making a note of your reasoning. Can you work out what happens from hints in the narrative, or do your answers rely on your own knowledge of the world, relationships and so on?

- When you have finished the chapter, join up with another student and compare questions and answers.

After reading Chapter 3

Annotating fragments

Included here are some short quotations from Chapter 3. Cut them up and stick them on a big sheet of paper with space around each one for annotations, as shown in the example.

- Annotate each fragment to show what it suggests about:
  - the nature of the novel
  - the presentation of childhood
  - the use of humour
  - the use of suspense.

A child's sense of adventure.

> I can see all kinds of interesting new possibilities opening up [...] (*Page 37*)

Present tense makes you feel as though you are back with the child.

Naïvety of the child's failure to realise the implications if she were a spy.

---

1. A father in the Secret Service *and* a mother who's a German spy [...] (*Page 37*)

links with stories
jealousy – child's perspective

2. I'm slightly regretful, though. I think of all the lemon barley and chocolate spread I've had from her [...] (*Page 38*)

sees things from own point of view – not big picture
childhood delights

3. I have private reservations about the spelling, but keep them to myself, as I do all the other small occasional reservations I have about his authority. (*Page 40*)

we want to know about here

4. Everything that we'd once taken for granted now seems open to question. (*Page 41*)

turning point
present tense

Studying *Spies*

Reading the Novel – Chapter 3

Quote	#
In the absence of anyone else I should for once be prepared to exchange a few words with Barbara Berrill. (*Page 43*)	5
The consequences of this investigation, I'm beginning to see, are going to be rather sad for all of us. (*Page 44*)	6
But then what can we do, if she's a German spy? We have to make sacrifices for the War Effort. We have to endure hardships for the sake of the Duration. (*Page 44*)	7
The grandmother clock ticks. There's no other sound. I wish I were back at home. (*Page 45*)	8
[...] all four of them watch us out of the past as we work to penetrate the secrets of the present and dismantle their future. (*Page 47*)	9
She actually *is* a German spy. (*Page 49*)	10
There's something she does once a month. Something she has to keep track of. Some secret thing. What is it? (*Page 49*)	11
But it's difficult to know what sort of look would be appropriate for talking to someone who we know has just had a secret rendezvous with a German courier. (*Page 51*)	12
But outside the house there's only one place where we can talk without being observed or overheard, and once we get there we're across the frontier into another country altogether. (*Page 52*)	13
I find it very difficult now to reconstruct what I'm feeling – it's so large and complex. (*Page 52*)	14
We've been entrusted with a great task. We have to defend our homeland from its enemies. (*Page 53*)	15
[...] our most secret and sacred possession – the bayonet with which his father killed the five Germans. (*Page 55*)	16
His face is set and pitiless. He looks like his father. (*Page 57*)	17
PRIVET, it says. (*Page 57*)	18

© English and Media Centre, 2005 — Studying *Spies* — 25

Reading the Novel – Chapter 3

Drawing the relationships

- Draw a diagram to show what you already know about the relationships between the different characters in *Spies*, as shown below. As you continue to read the novel, add to the diagram to reflect your developing knowledge.

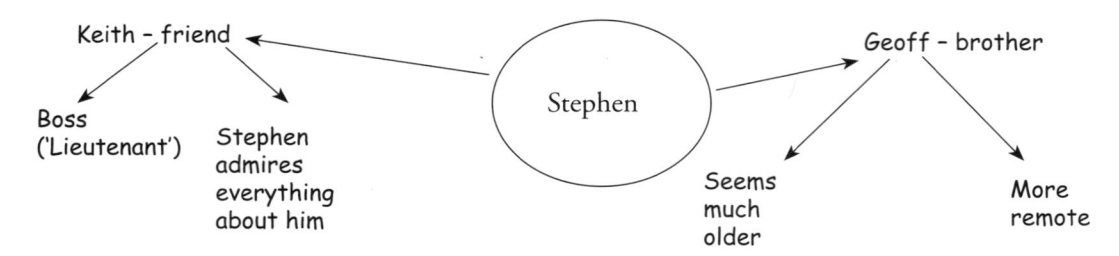

```
Keith – friend ←————————→ Stephen ————————→ Geoff – brother
     ↓           ↓                               ↓              ↓
  Boss       Stephen                          Seems          More
('Lieutenant')  admires                       much           remote
             everything                       older
             about him
```

Adding to the locations map

- If you have already started to draw a map of the Close and the surrounding areas, use Chapter 3 (particularly page 71 of the novel) to help you add to or amend what you have done so far. Annotate the map with key events and quotations, as well as any questions you have. If you have not yet started to draw a map, do so now, looking back through Chapters 1 and 2, as well as Chapter 3.

- In groups, or as a class, spend a few minutes looking at the different representations of the Close, questioning anything which doesn't seem to fit the details from the story.

- Take it in turns to suggest why the setting and layout of the area might be significant to the themes, as well as the plot, of *Spies*.

- Continue to work on your map as you read the rest of the novel.

A screenplay

At the time Michael Frayn gave the interview he was busy drafting the screenplay of *Spies*. In the interview he spoke about the difficulty of translating a literary text into a visual one.

> I am just at the moment writing a screenplay for the film version of the book, and of course the one thing you can't do in the cinema is have smells, so we've got to find some equivalent way of evoking the feel of that street, which doesn't actually involve the smells of the bushes and the trees.
>
> I hope we have found another way of doing it, but of course in the end, with film, it does all come down to what you actually see in front of you on the screen, and at the stage when you are writing the script, that's still quite an open question. You have still got to find the location, you have still got to find the actors that are going to embody those characters, and you have still got to design the location, and make it look like the location in the story.

You are going to re-write a short section of the novel as a screenplay.

- Read pages 44 to 49 again (from '"You chaps have got things"' to She is quite literally ... a German spy.'), making notes in the margin with your ideas about how you might convey the plot, mood, themes and relationships through the medium of film.

- Choose the section you want to work on and write a draft of the screenplay.

- Annotate your draft to show how you have used film language and techniques to get across what is created and conveyed in the writing.

- Talk about the qualities of the text that make it either easy or difficult to realise as a film. What have you now learned about Frayn's style?

Reading the Novel – Chapter 4

Chapter 4

During reading Chapter 4

Becoming an expert

- In pairs, or small groups, focus on one of the following aspects of the text as you read. You will be teaching this aspect of the chapter to the rest of the class.
    - Childhood relationships
    - Perception
    - The mystery of Mrs Hayward
    - The presentation and role of the male characters
    - The presentation and role of the female characters
    - Families

- After reading the chapter, prepare a presentation and take it in turns to give these to the rest of the class.

All a game?

From the very moment Keith reflects 'My mother is a German spy' there is uncertainty over whether this is part of a game, the latest in a long line of projects, or something more serious. The accusation, the act of spying, who is being spied on and by whom, and the implications for the characters involved are all perceived and treated in different ways.

- As you read Chapter 4, make a note of how serious the boys' spying is for different characters (for example Mr Wheatley, Auntie Dee, Mrs Hayward, Geoff and so on). Record the reasons for your thinking, with close reference to the text.

After reading Chapter 4

Narrative voice – adding to your chart

- If you began to fill in the narrative voice grid on page 11 of the study guide, add to it anything you have noticed in Chapters 3 and 4. If you have not yet started it, now would be a good time to look over what you have read so far, thinking about the shifting points of view and the different narrative voices.

The Haywards and the Wheatleys

Included on pages 28-29 are some short quotations about Stephen, Keith and their families. They are taken from Chapters 2 to 4 of the story.

- Read the quotations and annotate them to show what they reveal about the families and Stephen's feelings about them, both as a child and as an old man.

- Share your ideas in class discussion.

- Now watch Michael Frayn talking about social class and status in the novel.

- Bear in mind the points raised in your discussion as you continue to read, thinking about the importance of family, identity and status in the story of Stephen and in the novel more generally.

Reading the Novel – Chapter 4

Chapter 2

> Does he know, even at that age, what his standing is in the street? He knows precisely, even if he doesn't know that he knows it. In the very marrow of his bones he understands that there's something not quite right about him and his family […] (*Page 13*) **1**

> I was acutely aware, even then, of my incomprehensible good fortune in being Keith's friend. Now I think about it with adult hindsight it seems more surprising still. Not just his belt but everything about him was yellow and black; everything about me was plainly green and black. He was the officer corps in our two-man army. I was the Other Ranks – and grateful to be so. (*Page 16*) **2**

> One possibility, though, is too outlandish ever to be mooted – the idea of going to play at Stephen's house […] I try to imagine the impossible happening, and Keith asking his mother if he might play at Stephen's house […] I laugh at the thought. (*Page 19*) **3**

> The Haywards were impeccable. And yet they tolerated Stephen! (*Page 23*) **4**

> Stephen's father and Keith's presented a particularly piquant contrast. […] And even when he was at home he didn't whistle that terrifying whistle, he didn't call Stephen 'old bean' and threaten to cane him. He said very little. He often seemed like some mild-natured furry animal […] His appearance was as unsatisfactory as Stephen's. (*Pages 26-27*) **5**

Chapter 3

> I think I feel a brief pang of admiring jealousy for yet another demonstration of his unending good fortune. A father in the Secret Service *and* a mother who's a German spy – when the rest of us can't muster even one parent of any interest! (*Page 37*) **1**

Reading the Novel – Chapter 4

> Just the self-contained perfection of the house itself, the effortless superiority which the other houses in the Close can only recognise and defer to. (*Pages 43-44*) — 2

> I feel more strongly than ever the honour of my association with Keith. His family have taken on the heroic proportions of characters in a legend – noble father and traitorous mother playing out the never-ending conflict between good and evil, between light and dark. Now Keith himself is charged by fate with taking his place beside them, upholding the honour of the one by punishing the dishonour of the other. And I have been granted a modest foothold of my own in the story, as the loyal squire and sword-bearer that a hero requires. (*Page 53*) — 3

Chapter 4

> What *I* want to know, though, is why there's something awkward about going out to play on Friday evenings. Why my father has never killed any Germans. Why no one in the whole of my family is in the RAF. Why we have an embarrassing name like Wheatley. Why we can't be called something more like Hayward. There's something sad about our life, and I can't quite put my finger on what it is. (*Page 64*) — 1

> It's already getting near bedtime before I can slip away from my unsatisfactory family at last, and rush headlong out of the house. (*Page 64*) — 2

> Why does Keith have an aunt living three doors away? Aunts don't live in the same street as you! [...] And Keith's mother goes to see her not two or three times a year, but *every day*. (*Page 69*) — 3

> 'You know the rules. You know when you're supposed to be in. If you behave like a child then Daddy's going to treat you like a child.' (*Page 82*) — 4

Reading the Novel – Chapter 4

Characters in the foreground

In this chapter the reader learns more about Uncle Peter and meets Barbara Berrill for the first time.

- In pairs, talk about:
    - your impressions of Barbara and Uncle Peter and how these are formed
    - Stephen's responses to the two characters and how Frayn conveys these to the reader
    - your first thoughts about the role these characters might play in the story. You should think about the themes and ideas being explored, as well as the plot.

A spy story? A ghost story? Or something else?

As Stephen and Keith puzzle over Mrs Hayward's disappearance and reappearance Stephen comments, 'Perhaps it's not a spy story we've woven ourselves into, after all. It's a ghost story.' To help you develop a clearer sense of the defining features and conventions of different genres and how Michael Frayn draws on these, work through the following activities.

- Based on your memory of what you have read so far, suggest different genres that *Spies* draws on (for example, spy, ghost, mystery, adventure).

- Look back through the text, identifying short quotations which illustrate this. Talk about how you identified the genre (for example language, characterisation, setting, plot).

- What is the effect of Michael Frayn combining features and conventions from a range of genres?

There is more detailed work on genre in 'After Reading' (page 75).

Reading the Novel – Chapter 5

Chapter 5

Before reading Chapter 5

- On your own, write two or three sentences summing up what has happened so far in *Spies*.

- Now note down any themes or ideas which you are becoming aware of in the story. For each one, briefly explain the way Frayn explores it and why you think it is important.

- Compare your notes with those of one or two other people.

Reading Chapter 5

A shift in perspective

Chapter 4 ends with the line 'The dark of the moon's coming, and it's going to be more frightening than we thought.' told in the present tense, in the voice of Stephen as a young boy. Chapter 5 opens in the voice of the old man narrator with the comment, 'Everything is as it was; and everything is changed.'

- Read the first section of Chapter 5, up to 'Once again I try to wipe the dark-green slime off my hands.' (page 89) and talk about the effect of this opening on you. Why do you think Frayn chose to shift the perspective from the wartime story of Stephen's childhood to sixty years later and his return to the Close?

A close focus on style

Printed on page 32 of the study guide is a short extract from early on in Chapter 5.

- Read the passage and share what strikes you about it. You might comment on:

    – lexis (word choice)

    – rhythm

    – narrative voice

    – tense (past, present, future)

    – the relationship between memory, imagination and present reality

    – connections with the story of Stephen

    – effect on the reader.

Clues

In the same way that Stephen and Keith attempt to piece together the mystery of Mrs Hayward's disappearances and the secrets of her spying, so the older narrator (and the reader) tries to piece together his memories of this summer and its significance in his life.

- In pairs, or as a class, collect together anything which you think might be a clue in working out what really happened during the spying summer. Annotate your clues with any ideas you have about their possible significance.

© English and Media Centre, 2005   Studying *Spies*

Reading the Novel – Chapter 5

An extract from Chapter 5 – a close focus on style

The sound changes again as it crosses the bridge … and once again I hear the rumbling hollowness of the old brick tunnel as a train went over, and the never-ending returns of the high cries that Keith and Stephen uttered to test the echoes and show they weren't afraid, as they made one of their rare ventures through that long, low darkness.

Once again I glimpse the perils that lay beyond that echoing ordeal, where the old world resumed after the brief interruption of our familiar streets and houses, as indifferent to them as if they'd never been. We called it the Lanes, though there was only one of them, and so narrow that it almost disappeared in summer into the gross greenery of the hedgerows on either side and the shadows of ancient, crooked trees. I see the Cottages, the sly tumbledown hovels lurking behind the undergrowth in a debris of rusty oil drums and broken prams. I hear the barking of the misshapen dogs that rushed out at us as we passed, and I feel the sullen gaze of the raggedy children who watched us from behind their wicket gates. I smell the sour, catty stink of the elders around the collapsed and abandoned farm where you could sometimes glimpse an old tramp holed up, heating a blackened billy over a little fire of sticks…

Beyond the abandoned farm was a desolate no man's land half marked out as builder's lots, where colonisation approaching from the next settlement along had been halted for the Duration. Between the line of the railway and the wasteland of the lots, preserved for a few more years by the shifting tides of history, the last pocket of the rural world pursued its ancient, secret life. Each of the rare excursions we made into it was a frightening adventure, a series of ordeals to test our coming manhood.

And the first of the ordeals was the tunnel itself. Once again I hear our uneasy cries drowned by the huge thunder of the train passing overhead. Once again I see the circle of unwelcoming daylight at the end doubled by its reflection in the great lake that collected inside the tunnel after rain. Once again I feel the awkward twist of my body as I turn to edge sideways along the narrow causeway left at the edge of the lake, and simultaneously lean away from the glistening, dripping wetness of the brickwork. Once again I feel the dank touch of the walls on my hair and shoulder, and brush at the foul exudations they've left. Once again I try to wipe the dark-green slime off my hands.

Pages 88-89

Reading the Novel – Chapter 5

Before reading on – the tunnel

- As a class, share ideas about how you can tell that one person is more dominant than another in a relationship. Use the ideas suggested here to get your discussion started:
  - silence
  - apologising
  - staring
  - avoiding eye contact.

The next section of the novel (pages 89-94) is told in the present tense from the point of view of the younger Stephen. All the dialogue from this section is reprinted below.

- In pairs, read the dialogue aloud, then talk about what is happening in the story and what you can tell about the two boys and their relationship. Look closely at the dialogue to find reasons for your interpretations and suggestions.

Stephen:	She may have a transmitter hidden here somewhere. Or there may be some kind of secret research laboratory that she's spying on.
Stephen:	She can't be going very far. She always gets back almost at once.
Keith:	She's spying on the trains.
Stephen:	And she comes to this end of the tunnel…
Keith:	… so that no one sees her. She's probably got some special place to hide.
Stephen:	Perhaps we should go back.
Stephen:	We don't want her to see us here…
Stephen:	She can't have gone as far as that. She's always back too soon.
Keith:	She could be gradually assembling something. Bit by bit. A bomb. She's waiting for a particular train. With something special on it. A new kind of plane.
Stephen:	Keith? What are you doing? Where are you?
Stephen:	What? What is it?
Stephen:	We'd better tell Mr McAfee.
Stephen:	Or your father.
Stephen:	Don't! Don't touch it!
Stephen:	It might be the stuff for blowing up the train. Or it could be booby-trapped.

- Now read the full passage as Frayn wrote it. Is the passage mainly:
  - description
  - narration
  - reflection
  - commentary
  - dialogue?

- Talk about what, if anything, the description, reflection and so on add to your understanding of the situation and the relationships between characters.

© English and Media Centre, 2005 — Studying *Spies*

Reading the novel – Chapter 5

After reading Chapter 5

What is the chapter about? Finding evidence

Included here are ten statements summing up something about Chapter 5.

- For each one find either three pieces of evidence in support of the statement or, if you disagree with the statement, find three pieces of evidence which challenge it.

1. This chapter draws heavily on the conventions of the thriller genre.

   a. being followed
   b. escape from train in tunnel
   c. spying on spies footprint

2. In this chapter things become more serious.

   a. S. almost threatened by Mrs H. — uses code of honour
   b. Other spies — real punishing of lady S.J.
   c. Mrs. H. has S.J. to hide

3. Frayn encourages the reader to feel sympathy for Mrs Hayward.

   a. She's become more human whilst retaining mystery
   b. She's freer outside of house
   c.

4. In this chapter Stephen has increasingly to deal with events on his own.

   a. his encounter w/ Barry
   b. " " w/ Mrs H
   c. his dreams

5. This chapter is about humiliation.

   a. Stephen at hand of Keith
   b. BB
   c. Mr. H — protects sense of dignity

Reading the novel – Chapter 5

6. The children's view of adult lives is distorted.

   a. ....

   b. ....

   c. ....

7. Although the chapter deals with serious themes, there is still humour, particularly in Stephen's misunderstanding of the adult world.

   a. p.103

   b. How can someone old have a boyfriend?

   c. p.95

8. The chapter is about friendship.

   a. the ways some friendships work – diminished / led

   b. ....

   c. ....

9. This chapter is about betrayal.

   a. S. feels he has betrayed K.

   b. B.B. talks @ betrayal of husbands by wives taking lovers

   c. ....

sexual awakening of Stephen

10. The adult characters have very little idea of what is happening in the children's lives.

    a. Disagree. Mrs H knows S is watching + how to stop him

    b. Presumably adults do not know that B knows

    c. Mr H. appears to misread K – but is this a front

- If your interpretation of the chapter is not represented in the statements, write your own and find three pieces of evidence in support of it.

- When you have all your evidence gathered together, get into pairs or small groups. Listen to each other's evidence, then agree on three statements which for you sum up what is most interesting or significant about this chapter.

- Feed back your group's ideas in class discussion.

Reading the novel – Chapter 5

Mrs Hayward and Stephen – writing a letter

The end of Chapter 5 marks one of several turning points for Stephen. Mrs Hayward's conversation with him is the first of many secrets he has to keep from Keith.

- Re-read this passage on pages 105-110 (from 'She's not carrying a basket, though;' to 'I make no move to follow.'), paying attention both to what is happening on the surface and to what Stephen is thinking and feeling about the conversation.

- In role as Stephen, write a letter to Mrs Hayward in which he sets her straight on his relationship with Keith and explores the anxieties and conflicts he is feeling.

A question of perception – creative writing and hotseating

In the interview Michael Frayn identifies the 'philosophical seed of this story' as 'the question of perception' – how we make sense of what's in front of our eyes.

- If you did the activity on 'Perception' in Before Reading, look back at your writing and notes to remind yourself of the issues and ideas it raised. If you didn't, it would be worth having a go at this activity before considering how Frayn explores perception in the novel (page 8 of the study guide).

- Work in small groups on one of the following characters:
  - Keith — Rob / Mark
  - Stephen — Lauren / Rachael
  - Barbara Berrill — Maxine /
  - Keith's father (Mr Hayward) — Rosie / Graham
  - Keith's mother (Mrs Hayward) — Stephanie / Amy D
  - Stephen's father (Mr Wheatley) — Amy N /
  - Stephen's mother (Mrs Wheatley) — LGY

[Hwk]

- You will be asked to introduce your character in role and to give your interpretation of the events related in Chapters 3 to 5. You will need to look closely at the text for evidence of what your character is like, their relationships and their understanding of what is going on. In some cases you may be aware that their view of events is mistaken or partial. Make a note of why you think this and what you think is really going on.

- Take it in turns to introduce your character and be hotseated by the rest of the class.

- De-brief the activity by talking about:
  - the different interpretations of what has been taking place
  - the limited understanding the characters have, their misunderstanding of what is going on and the way Frayn conveys this to the reader
  - the points at which the reader remains uncertain or confused and why such uncertainty might be a crucial part of reading *Spies*.

- You could use what you have learned during this activity to write short diary entries for the characters. Choose one of the key events from the last three chapters and write an entry which indicates each character's view of what is going on.

Motifs

Before reading Chapters 3 and 4, you brainstormed associations and the possible significance of some key motifs in *Spies*.

- Look now at the way these motifs (particularly 'x' and 'privet') are developed in Chapter 5 and what their function seems to be.

Reading the novel – Chapter 6

Chapter 6

Before reading Chapter 6

Writing the next section

You are going to write the next section of *Spies*.

- In groups, or as a class, brainstorm possible directions the story might take and your reasons for thinking this.

- Individually, write the next instalment in the story.

- Swap stories. As you read, annotate the story to show where you think the writer has been particularly successful either in continuing the story in a fitting way, or developing the characters appropriately, or imitating Frayn's style.

- If you have time, take it in turns to read a few of your stories aloud, identifying any patterns or common approaches that you notice.

Reading Chapter 6

Predicting and titling

- Read Chapter 6, stopping at the following points to predict what you think will happen next, first on your own and then in class discussion:

    - pages 113-115: ('What is it that wakes me?' to 'I must do it, though, I must.')
    - pages 115-118: ('Between the reflected disc' to 'into the booming darkness of the tunnel.')
    - pages 118-120 ('The Close, as I come running' to 'with a heavily darned heel.')
    - pages 120-125 ('Keith turns the sock over in his hands' to 'We hurry forward.')
    - pages 125-129 ('All summer afternoons in the Lanes' to 'the last place we're sure she reached: the Cottages.')
    - pages 129-132 ('We dawdle about' to 'neither of us led').

- Choose a title for each of these sections (including the last one on pages 132-133). Then make up an overall title for the whole chapter.

- Take it in turns to share and explain your section titles.

After reading Chapter 6

What does Stephen think now?

- Flick through the novel up to the end of Chapter 5 and estimate roughly how much of each chapter is told from the point of Stephen (the boy) and how much from the point of view of Stephen (the old man).

- Share what you notice with the rest of the class.

After the first section (ending at page 115 'I must do it, though, I must.'), Chapter 6 is told entirely in the present tense from the point of view of Stephen, the young boy.

- Talk about why you think Frayn made the decision to tell this section of the story without any commentary or reflection from the older narrator.

Reading the novel – Chapter 6

- On your own, choose one of the sections from this chapter (115-120, 115-118; 118-120; 120-125, 125-129, 129-132 and 132-133) and annotate it with the commentary or reflections you think the older narrator might have added. Look back at earlier passages told in the voice of the older narrator to remind you of the following:
  - the style in which these reflections are written
  - the sorts of things the older narrator is interested in
  - the older narrator's view of his younger self.

- Join up with other students who have added commentary for the other sections and take it in turns to read them aloud.

Friends and bullies

In the interview Michael Frayn says: 'Bullying, of course, is one of the themes of the book.'

Chapter 6 foregrounds the theme of bullying and the abuse of power by exploring it from a number of different angles and in relation to different characters.

- In groups, look back through Chapter 6 and identify all the different forms of bullying taking place. Who is the bully and who is the victim? Draw out any connections you notice between these bullying relationships.

- Feed back what you have discovered. As a class, write three or four sentences drawing together the way in which Frayn explores power relationships and bullying between both adults and children.

- You can watch Michael Frayn talking about friendship and bullying on the DVD.

Into the tunnel – close language work on the development of tension

Two of the passages in this chapter are particularly tense: the one in which Stephen goes to the tunnel on his own at night and the one in which the two boys bang on the corrugated iron in the barn. The two passages are re-printed on pages 39-41. You are going to begin by working in pairs on one of the passages.

- Re-read the passage, highlighting the techniques Frayn uses to convey tension and create a sense of fear and panic. A few of the techniques are listed here to start you off:
  - short sentences, including incomplete sentences
  - build up of clauses, reflecting panicky breathing
  - focus on a single point of view.

- Join up with a pair who has been analysing the other passage and take it in turns to present your findings. Are the same techniques used in the two passages? Do they have the same effect?

Reading the novel – Chapter 6

Passage 1

I should go through the darkness of the tunnel. On my own. And out into the moonlight beyond.

If only I had a knotted rope...

The white stillness goes on and on. I've never seen the world like this before.

Slowly it comes to me that I don't actually need a knotted rope. I could simply walk down the stairs.

Now I've thought the thought, I know I have to do it. I know I'm going to do it.

And at once I'm terrified. The summer night has become suddenly freezing. I start to shiver so uncontrollably that I can scarcely get the jumper over my head or the sandals on my feet. I can hear my teeth rattling together like dice in a shaker. Geoff stirs in his sleep, as if he'd heard them too. I feel my way downstairs, and through the kitchen to the back door. Very slowly I ease back the bolt, still shaking. I step silently out into the silver darkness, and become part of it.

Never in my life before have I crept out of the house in the middle of the night. Never before have I experienced this great stillness, or this strange new freedom to go anywhere and do anything.

I shan't have the courage to go through with it, of course. I shall die of fear before I get beyond the end of the street.

I must do it, though, I must.

Between the reflected disc of silver-grey behind me and the second one in front of me is a darkness whose shape is defined entirely by sound. The huge reverberations of the water plopping from the wet blackness overhead into the black water beside me merge into suites of scutterings and splashings trailed by unseen nocturnal creatures fleeing before the long echoes of my panicky breathing. In my terror I lose my footing on the unseen narrow causeway along the edge of the unseen lake, and have to keep touching the slime on the walls to steady myself. The slime is full of germs – I'm getting germs all over my hands.

And then at last I'm out into the open night again, and looking up in gratitude at that serene white face riding full and round above the railway embankment. The night's coming when I shall be out in the darkness again with no moon to whiten the world. And even as I think the thought, a cool breath of air stirs, and the moon sails behind a cloud. The delicate white world around me evaporates.

I stand stock still, mastering my new access of panic. Slowly I piece together a world of sorts from the different densities of blackness around me, and from a few small sounds. The stirring of the leaves in the trees along the lane. The murmur of the telegraph wires along the railway track above me.

I creep forward again. By touch I find the harsh brickwork of the retaining wall ... the rusty links of the wire fence ... the broken stalks of the cow parsley ... the metallic smoothness of the box and its embossed inscription.

I listen. The rustle of the leaves, the murmur of the telegraph wires. My own breath. The distant barking of the dogs at the Cottages in the Lanes. Nothing else.

I ease the lid open. The shiny underside as it turns catches a faint gleam of light from the clouds. There's no trace of any light reflected from the bottom of the box, though. I'm looking into blackness. There's something odd about the blackness – something wrong with the *sound* of it... What's wrong is that there *is*

© English and Media Centre, 2005   Studying *Spies*

Reading the novel – Chapter 6

no sound. The hard interior surfaces should give back a faint response to the tiny atmospheric breathings of the night, and no response is forthcoming.

I cautiously put my hand inside. The texture of the air seems to change and thicken around my fingers, as they sink into some substance that gives beneath them. I snatch my hand away.

What I felt, I work out with hindsight, as my surprise subsides, was a *softness*. A dry, cool softness. The box has something in it. Slowly I work out what it was.

Some sort of cloth.

I put both hands very slowly and carefully back into the box. Cloth, yes… A lot of cloth… Different sorts of cloth… Some of it smooth, some of it fibrous… A hem… A button… Another button…

Underneath my fingers now is something rough to the touch, with a pattern of ridges and furrows that seems curiously recognisable. I think I know what it is. I slowly ease my hand right round it to feel its underside and its width – then stop.

The texture of the darkness around me is changing a little. I look up, and see the suggestion of a luminous edge to the clouds overhead. At any moment the moon's going to come out again. But something else has changed, too. Something about the *sound* of the world…

I strain my ears. Nothing. Just the shifting of the leaves, the sigh of the wires, the coming and going of my breath…

I focus my attention back on the object I'm touching. The underside of it feels the same as the top. It's about as wide as my hand… Yes, I know what this is. I begin to slide my hand along it, so that I can feel the end of it to check, then stop again.

The sound that's changed, I realise, is the sound of my breathing. It's grown more complex. It no longer corresponds precisely to the rise and fall I can feel inside my chest.

I stop breathing. The sound of breathing continues.

Page 115

Reading the novel – Chapter 6

Passage 2

The sound of the train has died away. And now I do hear something. Coughing. Very quiet coughing. He's trying not to let us hear him. He's scared. Scared of Keith, scared of *me*. He's *that* low in the table of human precedence.

At once, after all my cowardice in the Lanes, I'm brave. I look around for an instrument I can use to make the old man a little more frightened still. 'What?' whispers Keith. I say nothing. I go across to one of the heaps of old pots and pans, and drag out a bent and rusty iron bar. I'm taking the lead for once. I'm showing Keith that he's not the only one who can think of plans and projects.

I reach out with the bar and tap gently on the corrugated iron above the old man's head. The quiet coughing ceases at once. He's prepared to suffocate rather than let us know he's there.

I tap again. Silence.

Keith looks round and finds an old, grey piece of wood that seems to have split away from a fence post. He taps on the corrugated iron with it in his turn.

Silence.

I tap. He taps. Still no response. Still the old tramp's holding his breath down there.

I bring the bar down on the corrugated iron as hard as I can. Keith does the same with his piece of wood. We rain blows down, until the iron begins to dent. The sound fills our heads so that we don't have to think about the inconclusive end of our expedition, and the prospect of going back to the Cottages. It fills the great desolation at the end of the Lanes with human purpose and activity.

If it's as loud as this out here, what must it be like *underneath* the corrugated iron? I can't help laughing at the thought. I can't wait to see the comical terror on the old man's face as he finally comes rushing out and we run off into the Lanes.

He doesn't emerge, though, and in the end we have to stop, panting and laughing too much to continue.

No sign of him. No sound, either, apart from our own commotion, and another train rattling indifferently by behind the trees. It's swallowed up in the depths of the cutting, and the great silence returns.

I remember the time when Dave Avery and some of the boys from round the corner shut poor Eddie Stott up in the dark in the Hardiments' garden shed, and then beat on the roof. I remember the unearthly animal sounds of Eddie's terror.

The silence from under the corrugated iron is even more unearthly. Not a cry, not a curse, not a breath.

Our laughter has ceased. I feel a sudden chill finger of anxiety touch my heart, and I know that the same sensation is afflicting Keith.

The old man's *not* dead, though. How could he be dead? People don't die from a bit of teasing!

They die from fear, though…

Keith throws down his piece of wood. I throw down my iron bar. We don't know quite what to do.

Why don't we go down the steps and look? – Because we can't.

And suddenly we both turn and run, neither of us leader for once, neither of us led.

Pages 130-132

Reading the novel – Chapter 7

Chapter 7

Before reading the chapter

Chapter 6 ends: '"Oh Stephen," she says sadly. "Oh Stephen!"' Chapter 7 begins: 'So how much did Stephen understand at this point about what was going on?'

- Talk about the narrative voice and style of this ending and beginning.

A little later, the narrator says: 'If Stephen understood anything at all about what was going on, then I think it was this:'

- Talk about what you think Stephen understands at this point, including what he thinks about Keith, Keith's mother, the man in the Barns and his own actions.

Reading the Chapter

- Now read on, up to the end of page 141 of the novel ('Everything really had perhaps gone back to what it had been before.') to see what the narrator says. Talk about:
  - why the narrator leaves us in so much uncertainty about Stephen's thoughts
  - what ideas Frayn raises in this first section
  - why Frayn moves backwards and forwards between the older narrator watching the boy in the house and Stephen's thoughts and feelings.

Before reading pages 142 to the end of the Chapter

The chapter ends with the words: '"Thank you, Stephen," she says humbly.'

- Predict what you think will happen in the chapter to lead up to this point, then read the chapter.
- Having read the chapter, talk about what did happen and your view of it.

After reading the Chapter

'All my betrayals and failures'

- On your own, list what you consider to be Stephen's betrayals and failures so far.
- Compare your list with those of other people and agree a final list.

Summing up the chapter

Below are some ways in which a reader might view this chapter.

- Choose the three that you feel best express your view.
  - Stephen increasingly isolated
  - Emotional cruelty/physical cruelty
  - Stephen drawn into supporting Mrs. Hayward
  - A new perspective on Keith
  - Developing the theme of perception
  - A shift from childhood game into sinister reality
  - The thriller elements of the story foregrounded
  - A shift in focus from Stephen and Keith to Stephen and Mrs. Hayward
  - An increase in emotional tension with the Thermos incident and the father

Reading the Novel – Chapter 8

Chapter 8

During reading Chapter 8

Barbara Berrill, Stephen and the reader

- Read up to page 162 of the novel ending with 'Life's going round in circles'. While you're reading this section, think about: what Barbara knows; what Stephen knows; what the wider group of children (Roger Hardiment in particular) know; what the reader knows.

- Try writing a short account of your interpretation of what's happening in the Hayward household at this time.

- Talk about which character's interpretation of events is closest to your own. What effect does this have? What's your view on Stephen's comment on page 157, 'I don't know anything about anything.'

After reading Chapter 8

Sequencing the events

- Sequence the events below in the order in which they occur in the chapter.

- Share out each of these sections of the chapter and in pairs, or threes, work on the section you've been allocated. Prepare a two-minute presentation on that section, focusing on the questions below.
    - Is your section comic or serious, or a mixture of the two? What makes you think this?
    - Is this a key moment (in terms of plot, character, theme, motif or mood)? In what way?

The policeman goes to Auntie Dee's house and the Haywards' house. The man has been seen again. The children speculate about what's going on.	1
Keith's mother comes into the lookout, with a letter, but leaves when she sees Barbara.	2
Barbara Berrill comes into the lookout and tells him all about Keith doing the shopping and her view of what is happening.	3
Stephen's view of the world is suddenly changed. The word 'Lamorna' sums up his awakening sense of romance and sexuality. He has a revelation that Mrs. Hayward isn't a spy and that it's all about her love for a German airman who's been shot down.	4
Stephen wants help from a grown-up. He goes home and considers telling his family but finds it impossible.	5
Keith's mother finds Stephen alone in the lookout and asks him to help her.	6
Barbara Berrill comes back into the lookout to talk to Stephen. They find a cigarette stub and realise someone's been in the lookout. Barbara tells him about Deirdre and Geoff. Stephen shows her the secret possessions and they smoke a cigarette together.	7

Reading the Novel – Chapter 8

A boxing match

You will be debating whether Chapter 8 is humorous or serious. The debate will be done as a 'boxing match'.

- Form two groups. One group will argue for, the other against.

- Prepare your points and choose one person to put your arguments in the 'boxing ring'. The ring will be two chairs at the front of the room.

- The two representatives will come to the front and begin to debate the question until the teacher calls the end of Round One.

- At this point, the 'boxers' should go back to their corners to get more ideas. The same person can go out for Round Two, or a new 'boxer' can be chosen.

- While the boxing match takes place, others should cheer on their boxers and think about good ideas and arguments for the next round.

- Keep going for three or four rounds, then step out of your roles in the contest and talk about which side of the argument was more persuasive, and why.

'On my own'

In earlier chapters, the focus was on Stephen and Keith. At the beginning of this chapter, the idea of Stephen being 'on his own' is strongly evoked.

- List some of the reasons he now feels so alone.

As the chapter progresses, Keith seems to have been replaced by Barbara Berrill and later still, Stephen begins to see himself as part of the 'mob' of children, set apart from Keith.

- Talk about Stephen's feelings about these shifts:
    – his friendship with Keith and what's happened to it
    – feeling alone with his knowledge of Mrs. Hayward's activities
    – having Barbara enter into his world (as a friend? as a girl? liked? disliked?)
    – being part of the gang of children.

Secrets and betrayals

- Go back to your list of betrayals, made when reading Chapter 7. Add to them any fresh betrayals from this chapter, then, in pairs, discuss which of the betrayals you think Stephen feels most guilty about.

- List all the characters in this chapter who are keeping something secret. For instance, what is Geoff's secret, at the beginning of the chapter?

Chapter 9

Before reading Chapter 9

What does Stephen believe?

- As a class, remind yourselves of what Stephen now believes about Mrs Hayward and the man in the Barns.

What does Mrs Hayward want?

Chapter 8 ends with Mrs Hayward returning to the lookout to ask Stephen a favour:

> 'Stephen,' says Keith's mother quietly, 'now you're alone … I want to ask you to do something for me. May I come in?' (*Page 171*)

- In pairs, speculate about what Mrs Hayward might want from him, then consider how Stephen might respond to her requests. Choose short quotations to support your different suggestions.

Certainties collapsing

One of the striking features of *Spies* is the way oppositions are set up and challenged (for example friend/enemy). The oppositions are both a way of structuring the novel and exploring key themes. In Chapter 9 Stephen, the young boy, says:

> […] I realise that the very things that seemed so simple and straightforward then are not simple and straightforward at all, but infinitely complex and painful […] (*Page 179*)

- As a class, talk about what he might be referring to here. How have the simple things in Stephen's life become complex and painful?

There is a longer activity on oppositions on page 74 in 'After Reading'.

Reading Chapter 9

The conversation

- Read the first section of Chapter 9, up to 'She hadn't just imagined it.' (page 177).

- Using the information you are given in this section and what you know of both Mrs Hayward and Stephen, role-play the conversation or script the dialogue for this section. Try to imitate the style Frayn uses for both characters.

- Continue the conversation or dialogue to include Stephen's response to her plea.

- Listen to one or two of the conversations or scripts, then talk about the insights the activity has given you into Stephen and Mrs Hayward and the way Frayn has created their characters.

The basket – Stephen's dilemma (pages 177-181)

- Either as a class, or in groups of three, read the next section of Chapter 9 aloud (to page 181 'L…a…m…o…r…n…a', with two students reading the parts of Stephen and Mrs Hayward and one person reading the narrative.

- Talk about what you think causes Stephen to change his mind and take the basket. Choose short quotations from this passage to support your argument.

Reading the Novel – Chapter 9

Barbara and the basket – reading pages 181-187

- Listen to this section being read aloud, then in pairs, or as a class, talk about how it fits into the context of the novel. Some of the points you might consider in your discussion are listed here:
    - the plot
    - the development of character
    - relationships between characters
    - the creation and use of the setting
    - the development of tension
    - the exploration of key themes (for example: growing up, secrecy, identity, bullying).

'Can I have a word with you, old chap?' – reading pages 186-190

- In groups, read pages 186-190, then prepare a tableau (between 4 and 8 freeze-frames) to represent your interpretation of this passage. Your frozen pictures should convey the relationships and the atmosphere, in addition to what is actually happening. You could choose to do this in an abstract way.

- Present your tableau to the rest of the class, then talk about what each group chose to foreground.

After reading Chapter 9

Loyalty and betrayal – a push and pull activity

In this chapter Stephen feels torn about who or what he should remain loyal to.

- In pairs choose one of the following characters or ideas to work on.
    - Stephen's family
    - Mrs Hayward
    - Keith
    - Barbara
    - Mr Hayward
    - The 'German'/man in the Barns
    - 'The War Effort'
    - England
    - Male heroism
    - Stephen

- One of you should make a list of all the points in favour of Stephen remaining loyal to this character or ideal. The other should make a list of arguments in favour of Stephen betraying this character or ideal. If you are working on Stephen write down at least one reason both in favour of him staying loyal to, or betraying each character.

- You can carry out this activity as either a drama or paper activity. If you are doing it as a drama activity, sit in a circle, opposite the student you have been working with. The students who worked on the character of Stephen should stand in the middle. Take it in turns to present, in role, an argument why Stephen should stay loyal to, or betray the character or ideal you have been working on. (For example, 'I am Keith. Stephen should remain loyal to me because I am his friend.') The students playing Stephen should take a step towards anyone offering a persuasive argument and away from those they don't agree with, explaining the reasons for their decision.

Reading the Novel – Chapter 9

'Just a minute'

Included here is a series of statements about Chapter 9. Your teacher will allocate a statement to each student.

- Your task is to prepare a one-minute argument either for or against the statement you have been given.

- Listen to each 'Just a minute' argument. After each argument, the rest of the class should challenge or further the points already made.

> Chapter 9 is about growing up.

> It is what is *not* said in Chapter 9 that is particularly frightening.

> In this chapter it becomes clear that this is not an adventure or a spy story, but a story about growing up.

> This is the chapter in which Stephen's values shift: he recognises the cruelty of Keith's father and the kindness of his own.

> In this chapter Stephen is forced to re-evaluate what and who he has been loyal to.

> In this chapter the wartime setting seems particularly important.

> This is the chapter in which the novel shifts from being a story about children to being one about adults.

A value for 'x'

In this chapter Stephen thinks he may have found a value for 'x'.

- In pairs, list all the different values or meanings that 'x' has been given in *Spies*. How successful do you think it is as a motif to draw together the themes and events of the novel?

- Add to your notes anything more you have discovered about the way other motifs (such as 'Lamorna') are used in this chapter.

'Stephen'

The chapter ends with the man in the Barns calling Stephen's name.

- As a class, speculate about the significance of this naming.

Reading the Novel – Chapter 10

Chapter 10

Before reading Chapter 10

Looking for clues

- As a class, brainstorm all the possible identities for the man in the Barns.

- In pairs, take one of these possible identities and look for evidence in the text which either supports it or calls it into question.

During reading Chapter 10

After the bayonet – thought-tracking

- On your own, do a quick read through of pages 212 to 216 from 'I try to slip into the house' to 'I resume my howling.', to get a sense of what happens.

- In groups of four, talk briefly about what strikes you in this passage.

Although the episode is told in Stephen's voice, from his point of view, the reader is given no insight into what he is thinking. The passage is dominated by the family's questioning of Stephen and his continued 'Silence.'

- Why do you think Michael Frayn might have decided to silence Stephen's thoughts at this point in the story?

In your groups you are now going to write the thoughts of one of the Wheatleys. Your teacher will tell you which character to work on.

- Re-read the passage, stopping to write thought-bubbles for your character at three or four points. This should take no longer than five minutes. Make sure everyone in the group has a record of your character's thoughts.

- Join up with the rest of the class and share your ideas about how this passage fits into the rest of the novel. You should think about: the presentation of characters, the voice, the themes (for example, family, loyalty and betrayal, bullying, identity, secrecy and revelation) and style.

'The game's finally over.' What happened?

- Listen to the final passage of Chapter 10 being read out loud.

- Share your first responses.

- On your own, summarise what happens in this final passage as a list of key points or a flow diagram. Use different colours to show:

    – the events which you think actually take place

    – Stephen's fantasies and speculations

    – the interpretation of the older narrator.

- Take it in turns to present your lists or diagrams. Talk about any disagreements or areas of confusion, referring closely to the text.

Reading the Novel – Chapter 10

After reading Chapter 10

A nightmare world

In the second half of *Spies* the tone becomes much darker. Several of the passages have a nightmare, surreal quality to them.

- Do a quick skim read of the passages listed here and add any others which you would also describe as 'nightmarish'.
    - The tunnel at night – pages 115-118 (from 'Between the reflected disc of silver-grey' to 'into the booming darkness of the tunnel.')
    - Stephen's sleepless night – pages 191-193 (from 'Nothing can happen in that darkness now, though.' to 'unable now to speak at all or even to shake my head.')
    - Taking the basket – pages 194-196 (from 'And once again I set out on that horrible journey.' to 'A single quiet word: "Stephen."')
    - The end of the 'game' – pages 216-222 (from 'I'm woken from the depths of a deep and dreamless sleep' to 'The game's finally over.')

- On your own re-read one of these passages more slowly, highlighting the features which create the nightmarish mood.

- Either as a class, or in small groups, take it in turns to introduce the passage you have been working on.

Hero or coward?

One of the key themes of *Spies* is heroism and its inverse – cowardice. What does it mean to be brave, a hero? What does it mean to be a coward?

Chapters 9 and 10 bring the theme of heroism into the foreground.

- Collect together short quotations from Chapters 9 and 10 which bring to the fore questions of heroism and cowardice.

- As a class, talk about whose views are being expressed (Stephen's? The older narrator's? The author's?) and what these are.

Reading the Novel – Chapter 11

Chapter 11

Before reading Chapter 11

What now? Predictions

Chapter 10 ends with the line 'The game's finally over.' There is only one short chapter left.

- Write down your prediction for how the novel will end, with your reasons.

- Listen to everyone's predictions before reading on.

During reading Chapter 11

A revelation

- Read up to the break on page 228 ('the raw, urgent reek of the privet faded').

The older narrator begins the next section of this chapter by saying:

> There were many things that Keith had been wrong about, I realised gradually as life went on. But about one thing, and one quite surprising thing, he'd been right [...]

- In pairs, talk about what this might mean. What might Keith have been right about?

- Read on to 'the terrible pull of opposites that torments the displaced everywhere'. Then stop again and share your response to what you have learned about Stephen. Look back through the novel for any clues or hints as to Stephen's identity.

- How does what you have learned fit with the rest of the novel? Does it make you reconsider your interpretation of Stephen's story, both as a child and as an adult?

This is what one critic said about the revelations you have just read:

> The unnecessary and empty suspense can't jibe with Frayn's insistence that the book be cast as a recollection. The same is true for the wilful naïveté of the child narrator. If we are not to benefit from the older man's perspective until the last dozen or so pages, why introduce him at the start?

- Do you agree? Talk about your response with the rest of the class.

- Now read the rest of the chapter.

What has happened to everyone?

In this chapter the old man Stephen recounts what has happened to his family, friends and other residents of the Close since the spying summer.

- Record the details of what has happened to everyone in the chart on page 51.

Reading the Novel – Chapter 11

Character	Stephen's speculations	Factual knowledge
Stephen		
Keith		
Mrs Hayward		
Mr Hayward		
Auntie Dee		
Barbara		
Geoff		
The Averys		
The McAfees		

■ Talk about the effect on the reader of these revelations about the fate of each person.

A personal response

■ On your own, write a few paragraphs exploring your response to the novel, and the way it ends. For example, you might think about:

– the way the final chapter fits with what has gone before

– its relationship with the opening chapters

– the questions that have been answered and those that have been left unanswered.

You might also consider the tone or mood of the final chapter, particularly in Stephen's recounting of what has happened to both the people and the places of the Close.

An appropriate ending?

Some of the mysteries of the novel and of Stephen's childhood are revealed in this chapter to have mundane – if tragic – explanations.

■ Does this make the final chapter an effective or ineffective conclusion to this story? In pairs, argue both sides then feed back your main points in class discussion.

Reading the Novel – Chapter 11

Back to the beginning?

Chapters 1 and 11 take place on the same day.

- Read the opening and concluding chapters again. Talk about what is similar and what is different, using the chart below to keep a record of your ideas.

- How well do these two chapters work as a frame for the story of Stephen, the boy?

Similarities	Differences

Reading the Novel – Chapter 11

Themes, motifs and repeated phrases

Throughout the novel key themes, motifs and phrases are repeated.

- Make a list of those you feel have been most important in the novel. Make brief notes on how these themes, motifs and phrases are developed and transformed in the final chapter.

- Share your ideas in class discussion.

Heimweh and Fernweh

- Read the following extracts in which the adult Stephen explores the concepts of *Heimweh* and *Fernweh*.

> It's the longing to be elsewhere that in Germany we call *Fernweh*, which is in my case also *Heimweh*, a longing to be home – the terrible pull of opposites that torments the displaced everywhere […] All that remains is the familiar slight ache in the bones, like an old wound when the weather changes. *Heimweh* or *Fernweh*? A longing to be there or a longing to be here, even though I'm here already? Or to be both at once? Or to be neither, but in the old country of the past, that will never be reached again in either place? (*Pages 234 and 229*)

- Talk about what you understand by these words and the concepts they describe. What insights do they give you into the novel and your response to it?

Summing up the novel

Here is how one reader summed up the novel:

> A novel of uncertainty, of half knowing, and half refusing to know, of half belonging, of things being quite and not quite.

- How far do you agree with this summary of *Spies*? In pairs, talk about the ideas it raises, looking through the text for evidence either in support of it or to challenge it.

- Now write your own statement which captures what the novel is about for you.

- Take it in turns to read out your statements.

After Reading

After Reading

An interview with Michael Frayn

There is an interview with Michael Frayn about *Spies* on the DVD. You may already have watched a few sections while reading the novel. Some of the other activities in 'After Reading' also highlight particularly relevant extracts. The interview is divided into sections. You could watch the whole interview, or do the activity below to help you choose what you're most interested in.

Questioning the author

- Before looking at the interview, decide which of these issues you would like to ask the author about, then go to the relevant sections (indicated in the brackets) to hear his answers.

    1. Where did the idea for writing the book come from? (1)
    2. Why choose *Spies* as a title? (5)
    3. Why focus on spying? (1b), (5)
    4. What's the main theme of the novel? (6)
    5. Does the book have any underlying philosophical ideas? (6)
    6. Do you think children are different from adults? (2a, 2c, 2d)
    7. What did you want to explore about childhood? (2)
    8. Can you tell us about Stephen's relationship with Keith? (2b, 2d)
    9. In what ways is the book about power relationships? (2b)
    10. Is class and social status important in the novel? (2d)
    11. In what ways is Barbara Berrill an important character in the novel? (7a, 7b)
    12. Were you drawing on your own experiences in writing this novel? (1a), (3), (4b), (7b)
    13. Why did you use two narrators? (8)
    14. In what ways is the novel about bullying? (2b)
    15. Is this a novel about growing up? (7b)
    16. Why do you use the motif of the privet? (9)
    17. Were you trying to explore differences between male and female worlds? (2b, 2c), (7a, 7b)
    18. Why write about Germany? (4b)
    19. In what sense is the book about identity? (4c)
    20. What were you trying to convey about wartime England? (3), (4a)
    21. How did you go about structuring and writing a novel like *Spies*? (10)
    22. Would it be different reading this as a German reader, as opposed to an English reader? (11a)
    23. Do you write with your readers in mind? (11b)
    24. Is this novel a spy thriller? How important is genre to you? (1b)

After Reading

DVD section headings
1. The idea of the book
    a) The germ of the story
    b) A spy story
2. Childhood
    a) Children's views
    b) Children and power
    c) Rules and expectations
    d) Status and hierarchies
3. Wartime England
4. England and Germany
    a) The Second World War
    b) An interest in Germany
    c) Dislocation and identity
5. Why 'Spies'?
6. The theme of perception
7. The female world
    a) Barbara and Mrs. Hayward
    b) The growth of sexuality
8. The two narrators
9. Motifs – the privet
10. The process of writing
11. Readers' responses
    a) German readers
    b) Writing for readers

The complete interview with Michael Frayn

A slideshow
1. Images from the 1940s
2. Book covers

After Reading

A response chain

- Write a short personal response to *Spies*, focusing on anything which you found particularly interesting, significant, confusing or irritating. Although this is a personal response you should still provide examples to illustrate your opinions through either quotation or close reference to the text.

- Pass your response to the person on the right of you so that everyone has someone else's opinions to comment on.

- Read the response you have been given, then write three or four sentences extending, challenging or commenting on it. You should make sure that you add at least one new idea of your own.

- Do the same another two or three times, then take it in turns to read out your response chains.

Spies – the title

- Now that you have read the book, talk about how successful you think the choice of title is. You might consider the issues suggested here.
    - Who is spying on whom?
    - What does the idea of spying represent and what themes does it raise?
    - The extent to which the title indicates the genre of the novel.
    - Michael Frayn's own comment that:

> I've called it *Spies* because it is about people observing each other.

Book covers

Page 57 includes four front cover images. Three were used as the front cover of the novel, The fourth (in the bottom left-hand corner) is the front cover of this study guide.

- Look closely at the four covers included here. Talk about the way the motifs and themes developed in the novel have been explored by the cover designers. What has been foregrounded? What has been marginalised? Why do you think this is?

All four covers are included in colour on the DVD.

After Reading

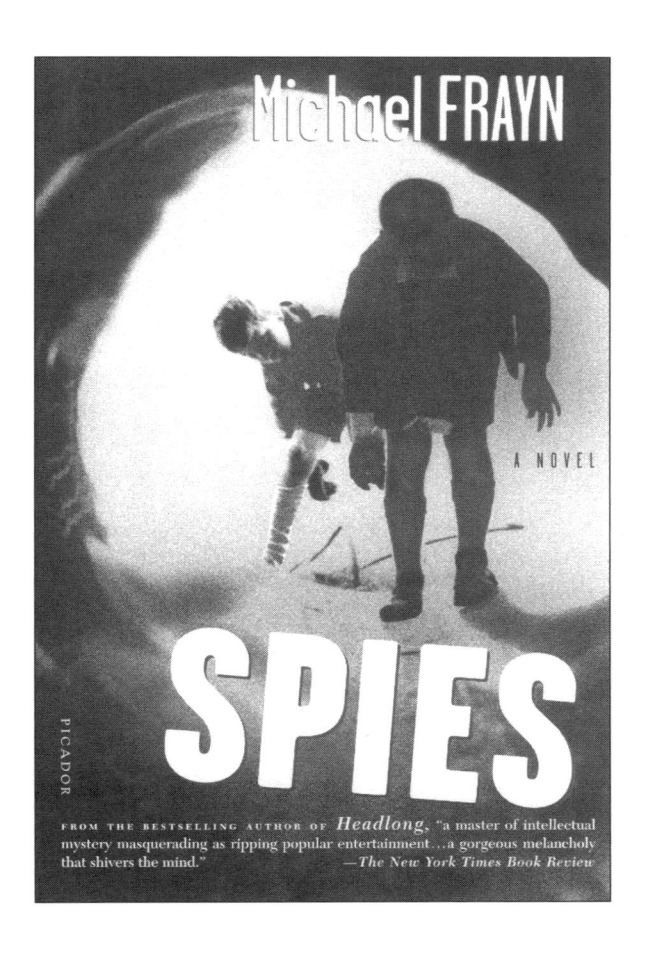

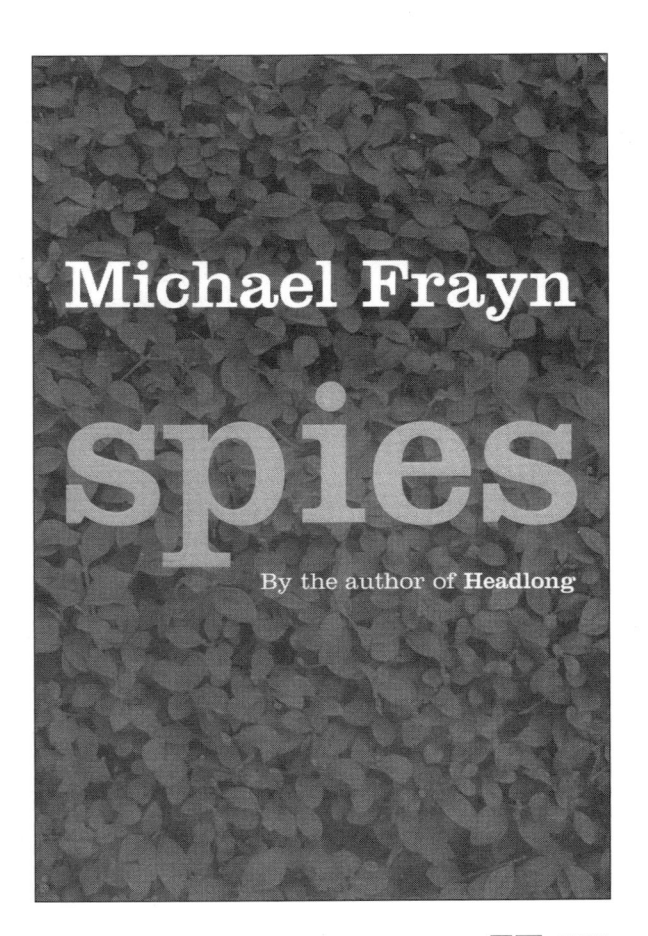

Studying *Spies*

After Reading

Male and female characters

You are going to explore the presentation and role of male and female characters and the ways in which these worlds are created.

- Read the extracts from the interview with Michael Frayn, included here. You can also watch this extract from the interview on DVD.

The female world – Barbara and Mrs Hayward

> The girl in the story, Barbara, is a little older than the boys, which gives her an advantage, but I think it is a commonplace of educational psychology that girls do tend to be rather ahead of boys in their intellectual development, and she just knows a bit more about the world than they do, and exploits this knowledge, partly to show off to Stephen, partly to tease him and partly because she is interested in him as another person. Mrs Haywood, Keith's mother, who is, I suppose, in some ways the central figure in the story, knows a lot more than anybody else, because she is the one with the secret. She has a secret world she is involved in, that she understands and knows about, and nobody else around her knows as much as she does about that world. Everybody else is guessing at it, making interpretations of it, some of them wrong, some of them right, but she is the one who knows.

The male world – heroes and myths

> Keith's father is mythologised by Keith, because he is such an uninteresting and horrible man. Keith builds up an entirely fictitious picture of him, as First World One hero, and a tennis champion. When he goes off to the Home Guard every week, his son says he's really a member of the Secret Service and the Home Guard is just a cover for his Secret Service activities.
>
> [...] Keith, of course, has been brutalised by his father – his father is a very cold and brutal man.

Listed below are some of the key male and female characters.

Male	Female
Stephen	Mrs Hayward
Keith	Barbara
Mr Hayward	Auntie Dee
Mr Wheatley	Mrs Wheatley
Geoff	Deirdre

- In pairs, work on either the male characters or the female characters, refreshing your memory of the role they play. Although you will need to consider the novel as a whole, you may want to pay particular attention to the following passages:

The male world: pp. 20-21, 22-23, 26-27, 96, 139, 186-189

The female world: pp. 20, 23, 40, 42, 96-102, 104-106, 104-106, 181-186

- Talk about the representations of masculinity and femininity provided by these characters and whether Frayn seems to be saying anything important about male or female behaviour. For instance, does he seem to be upholding ideals of male bravery and strength, or is he questioning them? Which of the male characters is most 'heroic' and what does that suggest about the values of the novel?

After Reading

A novel about perception

In the video interview, Michael Frayn suggests the novel is about perception and the way we all make sense of the world. This activity uses creative approaches to explore the different perspectives the characters have on what is happening.

Perspectives on the summer – the diary room

- Imagine each of the following characters has been asked to keep a video diary over the course of this summer:
    - Barbara
    - Stephen
    - Keith
    - Mrs Hayward
    - Mr Hayward

As a class decide who will work on each character.

- On your own, prepare brief notes to help you remember the main things your character might talk about in his or her video diary. You can choose to prepare either one extended entry in which you look back at what has been happening in the Close over the whole summer, or a series of shorter entries tracing your changing understanding as the events unfold.

- Join up with four students who have worked on the other characters. Take it in turns to do your video diary, with the rest of the group asking *Big Brother*-style questions to challenge or draw out the views being presented.

If you have access to a video camera, an alternative way of doing this activity would be to take it in turns to record all your diary entries, then watch them as a class.

- Feed back your most interesting discoveries, then talk about the different views the characters have of what is going on. What do these different perspectives contribute to the plot of the novel, the developing tension and Frayn's exploration of perception?

Growing up – a bildungsroman

Although *Spies* draws on a number of genres, for example spy story, romance, thriller (see page 75), it can be read as a novel about growing up – a *bildungsroman*. This is how a number of reviewers have interpreted it.

- On a line like the one shown here, record the points at which Stephen's experiences force him to grow up or to recognise something disturbing about the adult world. An example has been given to get you started.

- Then in a different colour, annotate the line to show how Michael Frayn conveys this.

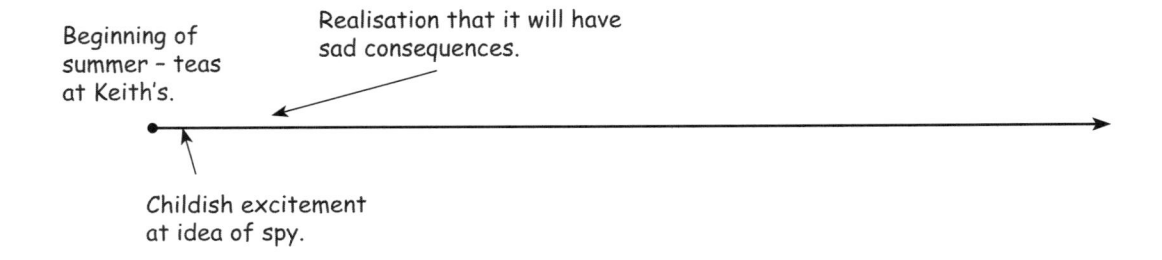

Beginning of summer – teas at Keith's.

Realisation that it will have sad consequences.

Childish excitement at idea of spy.

After Reading

Narrative perspective

One way of thinking about the structure of the novel is to think about whether the narrative is focusing on the older Stephen or on the child Stephen. Both narratives are told in the first person from the point of view of Stephen, as Michael Frayn indicates:

> I have used two narrators in the book, the two narrators being the same person, but at different ages, one as a child, and the same person when he is an old man looking back on himself.

First explorations – reading extracts

Before attempting to chart the shifts in the narrative perspective in the novel, you are going to explore a selection of short extracts from the novel.

- Read the extracts, annotating them to show the perspective from which the story is being told at this point. How would you describe the narrative voice (for example distant, close, reflective, reliable, intimate, puzzled, confident, uncertain)?

- Share your initial thoughts in small groups or as a class.

1

Another hint of it as the summer breeze stirs, and I know that the place I should like to be off to is my childhood. Perhaps the home I'm homesick for is still there, after all. I can't help noticing, as I do every summer in late June, when that sweet reek comes, that there are cheap flights to that far-off nearby land. Twice I pick up the phone to book; twice I put it down again. You can't go back, everyone knows that … So I'm never going, then? Is that what I'm deciding? I'm getting old. Who knows, this year may be the last chance I'll get …

But what *is* it, that terrible, disturbing presence in the summer air? If only I knew what the magic blossom was called, if only I could see it, perhaps I'd be able to identify the source of its power. I suddenly catch it while I'm walking my daughter and her two small children back to their car after their weekly visit. I put a hand on her arm. She knows about plants and gardening. 'Can you smell it? There… now… What is it?' *Pages 3-4*

2

I walk slowly up to the little turning circle at the end. The same fourteen houses sit calmly complacent in the warm, dull summer afternoon, exactly as they always did. I walk slowly back to the corner again. It's still here, exactly as it always was. I don't know why I should find this so surprising. I wasn't expecting anything different. And yet, after fifty years …

As the first shock of familiarity subsides, though, I begin to see that everything's not really as it was at all. It's changed completely. *Pages 9-10*

After Reading

> Stephen Wheatley … Or just plain Stephen … On his school reports S.J. Wheatley, in the classroom or the playground just plain Wheatley. Strange names. None of them seems quite to fit him as I watch him now. He turns back, before he slams the front door, and shouts some inadequate insult with his mouth full in response to yet another supercilious jibe from his insufferable elder brother. One of his grubby tennis shoes is undone and one of his long grey socks has slipped down his leg into a thick concertina; I can feel in my fingertips, as clearly as the scaliness of the snake, the hopeless bagginess of the failed garter beneath the turned-down top.
>
> Does he know, even at that age, what his standing is in the street? He knows precisely, even if he doesn't know that he knows it. In the very marrow of his bones he understands that there's something not quite right about him and his family, something that doesn't quite fit with the pigtailed Geest girls and the oil-stained Avery boys, and never will. *Pages 12-13*

3

> Stephen waits at the front door. Now, too late, he becomes aware of his appearance. He pulls up the sagging sock, and bends down to tie the untied tennis shoe. But already the door's opening a foot or two, and a boy of Stephen's age stands framed in the darkness of the house beyond. He, too, is wearing a grey flannel shirt and grey flannel shorts. His shirt, though, is not too short, his shorts are not too long. His grey socks are neatly pulled up to half an inch below his knees, and his brown leather sandals are neatly buckled.
>
> He turns his head away. I know what he's doing. He's listening to his mother ask who it is at the door. *Pages 14-15*

4

> Where the story began, though, was where most of our projects and adventures began – at Keith's house. At the tea table, in fact – I can hear the soft clinking made by the four blue beads that weighted the lace cloth covering the tall jug of lemon barley …
>
> No, wait. I've got that wrong. The glass beads are clinking against the glass of the jug because the cover's stirring in the breeze.
>
> [**]
>
> Or have I got everything back to front? Had the policeman already happened before this?
>
> It's so difficult to remember what order things occurred in – but if you can't remember *that*, then it's impossible to work out which led to which, and what the connection was. What I remember, when I examine my memory carefully, isn't a narrative at all. It's a collection of vivid particulars. Certain words spoken, certain objects glimpsed. Certain gestures and expressions. Certain moods, certain weathers, certain times of day and states of light. Certain individual moments, which seem to mean so much, but which mean in fact so little until the hidden links between them have been found. *Pages 31-32*

5

After Reading

> I'm dimly aware that my mother is fussing away on some familiar theme. I think it's her usual: 'You're not making a nuisance of yourself going over to Keith's house all the time, are you?'
>
> 'No,' I mumble, with my mouth full of semolina pudding; not something that Keith would ever do – or me either, if I were at his house.
>
> 'You're not going back there this afternoon?'
>
> I don't think I reply to this. I don't think I even look at her. There's something so hopelessly ordinary about her that it's difficult to take account of her existence. *Page 42*

6

> Keith sits cross-legged on the ground, his elbows on his knees, his head in his hands. I sit cross-legged opposite him, hardly conscious of the twigs sticking into my back or the tiny creatures dangling on threads that catch in my hair and fall down the neck of my shirt. I imagine my mouth's hanging half-open once again as I humbly wait for Keith to announce what we're to think and what we're to do. *Page 52*

7

> The last thing I see as she goes is her wiping her hands against each other. The brushing of her hair and the slapping at her shoulder were evidently an attempt to get some substance off them. Now it's on her hands, and it seems to be sticky and difficult to be free of.
>
> And suddenly I know what it is. It's not something sticky. It's something *slimy*.
>
> I know something else, too. I know where she's been each time she's disappeared.
>
> I shiver. The little marks in the diary are true. The dark of the moon's coming, and it's going to be more frightening than we thought. *Page 82*

8

> Everything is as it was; and everything has changed. The houses sit where they sat, but everything they once said they say no longer. The re-emergent greenwood has been uprooted and paved over. And Stephen Wheatley has become this old man who seems to be me. Yes, the undersized boy with the teapot ears, following his powerful friend open-mouthed and credulous from one project and mystery to the next, has become this undersized pensioner with the teapot ears, treading slowly and warily in the footsteps of his former self, and he has only this one final project and mystery left.
>
> A surprising thought comes to this old man, as he looks at the district now from the perspective of the years: that in those days all this was *new*. *Page 85*

9

After Reading

10

What is it that wakes me? Is it all my anxieties about the task we've taken on, and about what to do now that Keith's mother has told me to abandon it? Or is it my bad conscience about all the weakness I've shown and all the wrong thoughts I've allowed myself to think?

Or is it merely the unnatural lightness of my blacked-out bedroom?

There's a strange white light flooding around the edges of the blackout. I get up and slip my head under the blind. *Page 113*

11

Impressions… fears… But what did Stephen *make* of them all? What did he actually *understand*?

What do *I* understand? Now? About anything? Even the simplest things in front of my eyes? What do I understand about the geraniums in that tub?

[**]

I'm not sure, now that the question's been raised, if I truly understand even what it means to *understand* something. *Page 138*

12

I really have no idea, as I try to piece all this together half a century later, whether he understood or not. All I can remember is the chill that went through him at the sound. All I can feel now is his frozen paralysis as he crouched there with his satchel half on his shoulder, unable to move, to speak, even to think at all. *Page 199*

13

I walk up the street once more, to get full value from my air fare. One last look before someone calls the police or the local social services. Lamorna, I see, is now simply No. 6. Would the murmur of 'Number Six' ever have got as confused with the scent of the privet as the soft syllables of 'Lamorna' did? *Page 232*

14

Now all the mysteries have been resolved, or as resolved as they're ever likely to be. All that remains is the familiar slight ache in the bones, like an old wound when the weather changes. *Heimweh* or *Fernweh*? A longing to be there or a longing to be here, even though I'm here already? Or to be both at once? Or to be neither, but in the old country of the past, that will never be reached again in either place?

Time to go. So, once again – thank you, everyone. Thank you for having me.

And, on the air as I turn the corner at the end of the street, a sudden faint breath of something familiar. Something sweet, coarse, and intimately unsettling.

Even here, after all. Even now. *Page 234*

After Reading

Charting the narrative voices

- For this activity you will need to use any notes you have made on the shifts in the narrative voice. If you haven't been completing the chart on page 11 as you read, you will need to do a quick skim read through the novel, making a note of the changes in the perspective the story is being told from.

- Look over your record of the shifts in the voice and annotate it with any comments (for example anything distinctive you notice about the style of the narrative) or questions you have (such as why the older narrator refers to his younger self in the third person).

- In pairs, or small groups, talk about why you think Michael Frayn might have chosen to tell the story in this way. What do you see as the advantages and disadvantages of using this shifting perspective? Is there anything which confuses you or which you want to question further about the narrative voice?

- Take it in turns to feed back what you have learned so far about the narrative voices in *Spies* and the way these relate to the structure.

- Watch Michael Frayn discussing his decision to use a 'double viewpoint' in telling the story and talk about the insights you gain into the way the novel is structured. An extract from this discussion is re-printed below:

> One of the great difficulties I found in thinking how to write the story was from what viewpoint to tell it. If I told it from the child's viewpoint, it would, I think, rapidly become intolerable, that the child understood so little of the world in front of him, and if I told it entirely from the viewpoint of an adult, it would be very difficult to make sense of the child's view of the world, without seeming to be patronising. It was only when I thought of this double vision, of partly seeing it through what the child can understand, and partly seeing it through an adult trying to make sense of what the child could see, that it seemed to come together as a story.

The shifting perspective

Some critics have written explicitly about the shifting perspective. The four comments included here suggest that describing the novel as two first person narratives is too simple.

- Read the extracts highlighting what you consider to be the main points in each.

> **Critic 1**
> The book is deftly plotted, with the elderly Stephen commingling naturally with his younger self.

> **Critic 2**
> The unnecessary and empty suspense can't jibe with Frayn's insistence that the book be cast as a recollection. The same is true for the wilful naïveté of the child narrator. If we are not to benefit from the older man's perspective until the last dozen or so pages, why introduce him at the start?

> **Critic 3**
> [*Spies* is] the retrospective framework of a pensioner's reconstruction of his wartime childhood.

> **Critic 4**
> The sheer foreignness of childhood requires that he use the third person as often as the first.

After Reading

Some of the points you may have raised in your discussions are listed below.

- As a class, read and talk about the issues raised in these comments, amending or adding to them so that they reflect your views.
    - Although the focus shifts between Stephen as an old man and as a child, the reader is always conscious of the older narrator looking back on his life.
    - The childhood sections are like a film which the old man Stephen is listening to and watching.
    - Sometimes the older narrator tells the story of his childhood in the third person.
    - It is sometimes difficult to tell if the narrator is the adult Stephen looking back on his childhood self, or the child Stephen.
    - The sections about Stephen as a child are more like a story with dialogue.
    - Sometimes there seems to be another narrator observing the old man Stephen as well as the child Stephen.
    - Some of the childhood sections are narrated in the first person by the child Stephen; some of these sections are told by the old man Stephen as though he is a third person narrator.

Knowing and not knowing

Knowing and not knowing, secrets and revelations, ignorance and understanding, what is remembered and what is forgotten are all themes in *Spies*. Frayn draws our attention to these themes through the older narrator's repetition of 'I think' and his repeated questioning both of what his younger self knew and what he is now able to remember or piece together. As a result, the reader is also kept in a state of half-knowing, half-guessing uncertainty.

The reviewer from the *Daily Telegraph* comments:

> Far from being just a philosophical novelty, Frayn's ingenious treatment of perception gains extra moral weight when it comes to be about identity, and about the kind of double-think that people half-know is untrue, but go along with anyway.

- Talk about who is doing the revealing and concealing in this story and why. Use the statements below to get your discussion started.
    - The old man narrator knows more than he is prepared to reveal.
    - The child Stephen knows more about what is going on than he is prepared to reveal to himself.
    - Michael Frayn wants to keep the reader in suspense.
    - The old man narrator cannot remember exactly what happened.
    - It is only as he tells the story that the old man narrator remembers what happened.
    - The child Stephen does not want to acknowledge all he knows about Mrs Hayward and the man in the Barns.
    - Stephen is still trying to treat it all as a game.
    - Stephen never did understand what was going on as a child and he knows no more now he is an old man.
    - The older narrator knows everything that happened, but is choosing to spin out his story.

After Reading

Structure

The following activities focus on the structure of the novel – the way it is put together and sequenced. You will need to complete the first activity 'Segmenting the novel' before going on to attempt any of the others.

Segmenting the novel

- Draw a chart like the one shown below.

- Working on your own, divide the novel into 10-20 segments and give each of these a title. You might want to divide it into few large chunks, then sub-divide each of these into smaller sections (using the third column on this chart).

- Take it in turns to present your segmenting of the novel to the class. Talk about the similarities and differences in the ways you have each divided the novel into sections and the names you have given these.

Chapter	Main segment	Sub-section

After Reading

Patterns, shifts and repetition

One way of focusing on the structure of the novel is to trace the development and repetition of themes, ideas and key motifs to explore the importance played by different places and characters at different points. Some of these are included below.

- Before you think about their significance in the novel, cross out any that you don't agree with and add any others you think are missing.

- Draw a chart as shown on page 68 (or photocopy it onto A3). Use the work you have done on segmenting the novel to fill in column two.

- Fill in columns 3 to 7 to show which characters, themes, places, motifs and phrases are most significant at each stage of the novel.

- In groups or as a class, take it in turns to present your charts. Use your charts to discuss the way in which the motifs are used to structure the novel.

- How does Frayn balance the need to keep the story moving forward with the looping or recursive structure?

Characters
Barbara
Keith
Auntie Dee
Mrs Hayward
Geoff
Mrs Wheatley
Mr Wheatley
Mr Hayward
Uncle Peter
Other children
The policeman

Motifs
The smell of privet
Germs
Slime
Cigarettes
The word 'Lamorna'
The bayonet
The x's
Letters
The scarf
Photos

Words/phrases
'Lamorna'
'Everything is as it was and everything has changed.'
'On Stephen!'
'old bean'
'The game'
'bosom'
'satisfactory' and 'unsatisfactory'
'for ever'

Themes
Secrecy
Betrayal
Class
Ideas of male heroism
Male/female relationships
Loss of innocence
Continuity & change
Sameness & difference
Belonging

Places
The Haywards' house
The lookout
The Lanes
The tunnel
The Barns
Stephen's house
Auntie Dee's house
The shops
The post box

After Reading

Ch/pp	Segment	Characters	Themes	Places	Motifs	Words

After Reading

Chronological and narrative time

One way of thinking about the way Frayn has structured the novel is to compare the order things happen in the telling of the story (narrative time) with the order in which the events actually happened (chronological time). The chart below shows how narrative time relates to chronological time at the beginning of the novel.

- Working in pairs, look closely at this chart and fill in the third column with your comments on the relationship between narrative and chronological time.

- Still in your pairs, choose another passage in which you think the relationship between narrative and chronological time is particularly interesting. Complete a chart, like the one below. If possible, arrange for each pair to look at a different passage.

- Take it in turns to feed back your discoveries to the rest of the class. If you completed the activities on narrative perspectives in *Spies* (pages 60-65), you could compare the way in which Frayn manipulates both time and narrative voice throughout the novel.

- Talk about why you think Frayn might have decided to tell the story in this way. What insights do you gain into the way the novel has been structured and the effect this has on the reader?

The beginning of the novel

Narrative time	Chronological time	Comment
1990s: Smell of privet brings back a series of memories to an old man now living in Germany. ↓ Narrator speculates about Keith and Keith's mother. ↓ Old man decides he'd like to work out connections, uncover secrets. He decides to return to England. ↓ Arriving at the station. ↓ Seeing the Close again. ↓ Series of memories of his childhood. Reflecting back on what he was like as a child and what he knew. Teas at Keith's house. ↓ Keith's announcement ('My mother's a spy.'). ↓ Considering how he reacted to this news as a child. ↓ The boy Stephen regretting what this will mean – no more nice teas. ↓ The boys abandon their earlier game and begin spying. ↓ Old man sees the geraniums where the lookout used to be.	Series of summers 60 years ago in which Keith and Stephen played together. ↓ Teas at Keith's house. ↓ Keith's announcement: 'My mother's a spy'. ↓ Stephen regretting what this will mean – no more nice teas. ↓ The boys abandon their earlier game and begin spying.	

After Reading

Openings and endings

■ In pairs, brainstorm features and conventions of the beginnings and endings of chapters.

The first and last paragraphs from each chapter are reprinted below and on page 71.

■ Work in pairs. Half the pairs should focus on the openings; the other half should focus on the endings.

■ Read the paragraphs you have been given. Talk briefly about your first responses.

■ Read the paragraphs for a second time. This time look for patterns in:
- ideas
- themes
- metaphor
- narrative voice
- style (e.g. lexis, sentence structures and type).

■ Join up with another pair who has been working on the other set of paragraphs. Take it in turns to introduce your findings.

■ Look across the openings and endings. Draw attention to any patterns you notice.

Openings

1 The third week of June, and there it is again: the same almost embarrassingly familiar breath of sweetness that comes every year about this time. I catch it on the warm evening air as I walk past the well-ordered gardens in my quiet street, and for a moment I'm a child again and everything's before me – all the frightening, half-understood promise of life. (*Page 3*)

2 Everything is as it was, I discover when I reach my destination, and everything has changed. (*Page 9*)

3 So, she's a German spy. (*Page 37*)

4 She's hunched over a radio transmitter hidden in the cellars of the old castle, tapping on a Morse key, and I'm just about to spring out from behind the secret panel to confront her, when I realise that my name's being called, and I emerge from the shadows of the castle to discover that Mr Pawle is leaning against the blackboard with ironic patience, and that all the class are looking at me and tittering, as they wait for me to answer a question he's asked me; but what the question was, or even what subject we're doing, I have not the faintest idea. (*Page 61*)

5 Everything is as it was; and everything has changed. The houses sit where they sat, but everything they once said they say no longer. The re-emergent greenwood has been uprooted and paved over. And Stephen Wheatley has become this old man who seems to be me. Yes, the undersized boy with the teapot ears, following his powerful friend open-mouthed and credulous from one project and mystery to the next, has become this undersized pensioner with the teapot ears, treading slowly and warily in the footsteps of his former self, and he has only this one final project and mystery left. (*Page 85*)

After Reading

What is it that wakes me? Is it all my anxieties about the task we've taken on, and about what to do now that Keith's mother has told me to abandon it? Or is it my bad conscience about all the weakness I've shown and all the wrong thoughts I've allowed myself to think? (*Page 113*)	6
So how much did Stephen understand at this point about what was going on? (*Page 137*)	7
What's going to happen now? (*Page 151*)	8
I stop for a moment again in front of Meadowhurst. There's Stephen, the second tub of geraniums from the left. And there *she* is, Keith's mother, crouching beside him, the third tub. (*Page 175*)	9
Did Stephen understand at last who it was down there in the darkness, when he heard his own name spoken? (*Page 199*)	10
Everything in the Close is as it was; and everything has changed. The houses sit where they sat, but everything they once said they say no longer. (*Page 225*)	11

Endings

I certainly don't tell them the name of the shrub. I scarcely like to name it to myself. It's too ridiculous. (*Page 6*)	1
'My mother,' he said reflectively, almost regretfully, 'is a German spy.' (*Page 33*)	2
I don't like to query this, now that he's written it so neatly and authoritatively. In any case, the sense of it is plain enough – that we're commencing a long journey on a lonely road where no one else can follow. (*Page 57*)	3
I shiver. The little marks in the diary are true. The dark of the moon's coming, and it's going to be more frightening than we thought. (*Page 82*)	4
I make no move to follow. (*Page 110*)	5
'Oh, Stephen,' she says sadly, 'Oh, Stephen!' (*Page 133*)	6
'Thank you, Stephen,' she says humbly. (*Page 148*)	7
'Stephen,' says Keith's mother quietly, 'now you're alone … I want to ask you to do something for me. May I come in?' (*Page 171*)	8
And then, out of the darkness, his voice. A single quiet word: 'Stephen?' (*Page 196*)	9
The game's finally over. (*Page 222*)	10
And, on the air as I turn the corner at the end of the street, a sudden faint breath of something familiar. Something sweet, coarse, and intimately unsettling. Even here, after all. Even now. (*Page 234*)	11

© English and Media Centre, 2005 — Studying *Spies*

After Reading

Instant revision

Listed here are some of the main themes explored in *Spies*.

- Choose one of the themes (or come up with one of your own) and spend 10 minutes preparing a two-minute presentation on its importance to the novel.
- Listen to the presentations, then draw out any connections you see between the themes.

Englishness	Deception/betrayal
Power	Memory
Friendship	Identity (national, family etc)
Male identity	Perception/how we interpret the world
Conformity/individuality	Innocence and experience
Bullying	Sexual awakening
Storytelling/fantasy	Childhood
Belonging	The class system
Making sense of the past	Language and meaning
Alienation/dislocation	The role and place of women

After Reading

The pace of the novel – a debate

In his review for the *Guardian* Peter Bradshaw draws attention to the pace of the novel:

> The plot is like an aircraft [...] that spends a puzzlingly long time taxiing along the runway before it finally gets airborne. Even then it is only in the final 50 pages that Frayn pulls back the joystick, and with a great whoosh we are up for some very showy loop the loops and victory rolls [...]

- How far do you think this is true of *Spies*? Peter Bradshaw presents it as a criticism but could the slow start and the increasing escalation of the pace be interpreted as a merit of the novel? Spend just a few minutes making a note of your own response to the pace of *Spies*.

- Divide the class into two halves. One half of the class is going to prepare the argument that the pace of the novel works well; the other half is going to prepare a criticism of it.

- Your teacher will ask a representative from each half of the class to come to the front and argue the case. He or she will freeze the argument several times to give the debaters a chance to consult with the rest of the group.

Life as a story

In Chapters 1 to 4 Stephen is very aware of the power of Keith's imagination and of the story-like quality of his and Keith's lives.

- Annotate the following short extracts with your ideas about what is being suggested about:
  - imagination
  - the relationship between words and actions
  - childhood.

1. Spoken quite casually, like the most passing of remarks, as light and insubstantial as soap bubbles. And yet they changed everything.
   As words do. (*Page 6*)

2. I think now that most probably Keith's words came out of nowhere, that they were spontaneously created in the moment they were uttered. That they were a blind leap of pure fantasy. Or of pure intuition. Or, like so many things, of both.
   From those six random words, anyway, came everything that followed, brought forth simply by Keith's uttering them and by my hearing them. (*Page 33*)

3. I think I also understand that he's more than a protagonist in the events we're living through – that he's in some mysterious way their creator. He's done it before [...] In each case he uttered the words, and the words became so. He told the story, and the story came to life. (*Page 53*)

4. But the words will not imagine themselves. (*Page 54*)

5. I realise I'm tired of pretending to believe all the things Keith tells me. (*Page 68*)

6. Perhaps it's not a spy story we've woven ourselves into, after all. It's a ghost story. (*Page 77*)

7. The x's and the exclamation marks, too, have receded into the mists. They've become mere runes in an archaic text. (*Page 79*)

© English and Media Centre, 2005 — Studying *Spies*

After Reading

Challenging oppositions

One aspect of the structure and the themes in *Spies* is oppositions. Some of these are listed below.

- In pairs, choose one or two of these oppositions to explore in more detail. You should think about:
    - which of the terms in the pair is valued most and by whom
    - which characters are associated with which term in the pair
    - in what ways the oppositions and the values given to them are challenged in the novel, if at all.

- Feed back your findings and talk about any patterns you notice in the way the oppositions are established and challenged throughout the novel. How does Frayn use the oppositions to:
    - structure the novel
    - establish the setting and historical period
    - create character
    - explore themes
    - alert the reader to undercurrents, misunderstandings and absences in the text?

Oppositions

Germany/England	Brave/cowardly
Hero/villain	Male/female
Respectable/not respectable	Friends/enemies
Insider/outsider	Hero/villain
Loyalty/treachery	Adult/child
Private/public	War/peace
Trust/suspicion	Knowledge/innocence

After Reading

Genre

Spies and genre

The critic and reviewer Adam Mars-Jones comments that:

> *Spies* works as a mystery, as a war story and as a coming-of-age narrative. The only thing it can't quite be, despite its author's intellectual background, is a work of philosophy.

- As a class, share your first responses to this interpretation.

- Suggest other genres or types of novel with which you think *Spies* shares features, for example an adventure story.

- As a class, make a list of the main conventions and features of each of the genres you have suggested and those listed below. A few examples are included to get you started.

    Adventure – lots of events

    Mystery – gaps in the narrative

    War story – male-dominated

    Coming-of-age – reflective

    Romance – obstacles in the way of passion

    Novel of ideas – discursive passages

- In groups, choose one of the genres to explore in relation to *Spies*. Create a chart like the one shown here.

- Feed back your discoveries to the rest of the class.

Genre:		
Main features	**Ways in which *Spies* is similar/Quotation**	**Ways in which *Spies* is different/Quotation**

After Reading

Investigating genre

Included below and on pages 77-80 are extracts from a range of novels which might be seen to have something in common with *Spies* in terms of the generic conventions, the themes, the focus of the story or the narrative style and perspective. The titles and authors are listed on page 96.

- Skim read each extract, making a note of the type of novel it seems to be or the genre it belongs to. Highlight or underline anything which suggests this to you.

- In pairs, look in more detail at one of the extracts. Identify the features and conventions which indicate the genre or genres to which it belongs. Make a note of any ways in which it challenges or extends these genres.

- Think about how your extract relates to the way *Spies* is told.

- Take it in turns to feed back what you have discovered.

Extract 1

The best way to get to the British Museum would be to change at Notting Hill Gate and take the Central Line to Tottenham Court Road. Henderson shifted nervously in his seat as the train slowed, and watched Nunn May's dull image in the glass, waiting for him to pack up his paper and get ready to move.

But instead he was unfolding it on his knees.

The train stopped. Several people got off. The muscles in Henderson's legs were tense with the readiness to go. Nunn May carried on reading the paper. The doors closed and the train went on.

Bayswater. Nunn May stayed put. Paddington. Edgware Road. Henderson's legs were beginning to ache with their tautness. Baker Street, and still on.

We are on the Circle Line, thought Henderson. If we stayed on long enough we'd go right round and end up back in Kensington. And then we could still keep going.

Great Portland Street. Nunn May glanced up at the platform and began to fold his paper. The train pulled out of the station and trundled into the tunnel. Nunn May snapped his briefcase open –

– and put the newspaper inside.

Henderson stared in confusion, No copy of *The Times*. A ruse? He was getting out of his seat. The train pulled to a halt. Nunn May felt his way down the carriage, holding his briefcase and umbrella in one hand and keeping hold of the safety rail with the other. The doors opened. Henderson jumped to his feet.

Euston Square.

Henderson consulted his mind's eye map of London. It was, he realised, a perfectly sensible route. From Euston Square one could cross Euston Road and walk straight down Gower Street to the British Museum.

He let two men get off after Nunn May and then followed him out, his heart pounding painfully. The paper would come back out of the briefcase soon enough. It's now, he thought. It is finally going to happen.

And then he would be free.

After Reading

Extract 2

The past is a foreign country: they do things differently there.

When I came upon the diary it was lying at the bottom of a rather battered red cardboard collar-box, in which as a small boy I kept my Eton collars. Someone, probably my mother, had filled it with treasures dating from those days. There were two dry, empty sea-urchins; two rusty magnets, a large one and a small one, which had almost lost their magnetism; some negatives rolled up in a tight coil; some stumps of sealing wax; a small combination lock with three rows of letters; a twist of very fine whipcord, and one or two ambiguous objects, pieces of things, of which the use was not at once apparent: I could not even tell what they had belonged to. The relics were not exactly dirty nor were they quite clean, they had the patina of age; and as I handled them, for the first time for over fifty years, a recollection of what each had meant to me came back, faint as the magnets' power to draw, but as perceptible. Something came and went between us: the intimate pleasure of recognition, the almost mystical thrill of early ownership – feelings of which, at sixty-odd, I felt ashamed.

It was a roll-call in reverse; the children of the past announced their names, and I said, 'Here'. Only the diary refused to disclose its identity.

My first impression was that it was a present someone had brought me from abroad. The shape, the lettering, the purple limp leather curling upwards at the corners, gave it a foreign look; and it had, I could see, gold edges. Of all the exhibits it was the only one that might have been expensive. I must have treasured it, why then could I not give it a context?

Extract 3

'Are you ready to start off?'

'Yes,' said Julian, and began to scramble quietly out of his [sleeping] bag. 'We didn't tell the girls. [...] Now, let's be very, very quiet till we're out of hearing.'

Dick got out of his bag too. The boys had not undressed that night, except for their coats, so all they had to do was slip these on, and then crawl out of the tent.

'Which is the way – over there?' whispered Jock. Julian took his arm and guided him. He hoped he wouldn't lose his way in the starlit darkness. The moorland looked so different at night!

'If we make for that hill you can dimly see over there against the starlit sky, we should be going in the right direction,' said Julian. So on they went, keeping towards the dark hill that rose up to the west.

It seemed very much farther to the railway yard at night than in the daytime. The three boys stumbled along, sometimes almost falling as their feet caught in tufts of heather. They were glad when they found some sort of path they could keep on [...]

They went on for some way, and then Julian pulled Dick by the arm. 'Look,' he said. 'Down there, I believe that's the old yard. You can see the lines gleaming faintly here and there.'

They stood on the heathery slope above the old yard, straining their eyes. Soon they could make out dim shapes. Yes, it was the railway yard all right.

Jock clutched Julian's sleeve. 'Look – there's a light down there! Do you see it?'

The boys looked – and, sure enough, down in the yard towards the other side of it, was a small yellow light. They stared at it.

'Oh – I think I know what it is,' said Dick, at last, 'It's the light in the watchman's little hut – old Wooden-Leg Sam's candle. Don't you think so, Ju?'

'Yes. You're right,' said Julian. 'I tell you what we'll do – we'll creep right down into the yard, and go over to the hut. We'll peep inside and see if old Sam is there. Then we'll hide somewhere about – and wait for the spook-train to come!'

After Reading

Extract 4

He gave me a room at the back of the house, with a fine outlook over the plateau, and he made me free of his own study [...] I wanted some time to myself, so I invented a job for him. He had a motor-bicycle, and I sent him off next morning for the daily paper, which usually arrived with the post in the late afternoon. I told him to keep his eyes skinned, and make note of any strange figures he saw, keeping a special sharp look-out for motors and aeroplanes. Then I sat down in real earnest to Scudder's note-book.

He came back at midday with the SCOTSMAN. There was nothing in it, except some further evidence of Paddock and the milkman, and a repetition of yesterday's statement that the murderer had gone North. [...] I got rid of the innkeeper for the afternoon, for I was getting very warm in my search for the cypher.

As I told you, it was a numerical cypher, and by an elaborate system of experiments I had pretty well discovered what were the nulls and stops. The trouble was the key word, and when I thought of the odd million words he might have used I felt pretty hopeless. But about three o'clock I had a sudden inspiration.

The name Julia Czechenyi flashed across my memory. Scudder had said it was the key to the Karolides business, and it occurred to me to try it on his cypher.

It worked. The five letters of 'Julia' gave me the position of the vowels. A was J, the tenth letter of the alphabet, and so represented by X in the cypher. E was XXI, and so on. 'Czechenyi' gave me the numerals for the principal consonants. I scribbled that scheme on a bit of paper and sat down to read Scudder's pages.

In half an hour I was reading with a whitish face and fingers that drummed on the table.

I glanced out of the window and saw a big touring-car coming up the glen towards the inn. It drew up at the door, and there was the sound of people alighting. There seemed to be two of them, men in aquascutums and tweed caps.

Ten minutes later the innkeeper slipped into the room, his eyes bright with excitement.

'There's two chaps below looking for you,' he whispered. 'They're in the dining-room having whiskies-and-sodas. They asked about you and said they had hoped to meet you here. Oh! and they described you jolly well, down to your boots and shirt. I told them you had been here last night and had gone off on a motor bicycle this morning, and one of the chaps swore like a navvy.'

I made him tell me what they looked like. One was a dark-eyed thin fellow with bushy eyebrows, the other was always smiling and lisped in his talk. Neither was any kind of foreigner; on this my young friend was positive.

I took a bit of paper and wrote these words in German as if they were part of a letter -

... 'Black Stone. Scudder had got on to this, but he could not act for a fortnight. I doubt if I can do any good now, especially as Karolides is uncertain about his plans. But if Mr T. advises I will do the best I ...'

I manufactured it rather neatly, so that it looked like a loose page of a private letter.

'Take this down and say it was found in my bedroom, and ask them to return it to me if they overtake me.' Three minutes later I heard the car begin to move, and peeping from behind the curtain caught sight of the two figures. One was slim, the other was sleek; that was the most I could make of my reconnaissance.

The innkeeper appeared in great excitement. 'Your paper woke them up,' he said gleefully. 'The dark fellow went as white as death and cursed like blazes, and the fat one whistled and looked ugly. They paid for their drinks with half-a-sovereign and wouldn't wait for change.'

After Reading

Extract 5

And suddenly the memory returns. The taste was that of the little crumb of madeleine which on Sunday mornings at Combray (because on those mornings I did not go out before church-time), when I went to say good day to her in her bedroom, my aunt Leonie used to give me, dipping it first in her own cup of real or of lime-flower tea. The sight of the little madeleine had recalled nothing to my mind before I tasted it; perhaps because I had so often seen such things in the interval, without tasting them, on the trays in pastry-cooks' windows, that their image had dissociated itself from those Combray days to take its place among others more recent; perhaps because of those memories, so long abandoned and put out of mind, nothing now survived, everything was scattered; the forms of things, including that of the little scallop-shell of pastry, so richly sensual under its severe, religious folds, were either obliterated or had been so long dormant as to have lost the power of expansion which would have allowed them to resume their place in my consciousness. But when from a long-distant past nothing subsists, after the people are dead, after the things are broken and scattered, still, alone, more fragile, but with more vitality, more unsubstantial, more persistent, more faithful, the smell and taste of things remain poised a long time, like souls, ready to remind us, waiting and hoping for their moment, amid the ruins of all the rest; and bear unfaltering, in the tiny and almost impalpable drop of their essence, the vast structure of recollection.

And once I had recognized the taste of the crumb of madeleine soaked in her decoction of lime-flowers which my aunt used to give me (although I did not yet know and must long postpone the discovery of why this memory made me so happy) immediately the old grey house upon the street, where her room was, rose up like the scenery of a theatre to attach itself to the little pavilion, opening on to the garden, which had been built out behind it for my parents (the isolated panel which until that moment had been all that I could see); and with the house the town, from morning to night and in all weathers, the Square where I was sent before luncheon, the streets along which I used to run errands, the country roads we took when it was fine. And just as the Japanese amuse themselves by filling a porcelain bowl with water and steeping in it little crumbs of paper which until then are without character or form, but, the moment they become wet, stretch themselves and bend, take on colour and distinctive shape, become flowers or houses or people, permanent and recognisable, so in that moment all the flowers in our garden and in M. Swann's park, and the water-lilies on the Vivonne and the good folk of the village and their little dwellings and the parish church and the whole of Combray and of its surroundings, taking their proper shapes and growing solid, sprang into being, town and gardens alike, from my cup of tea.

Extract 6

The Outlaws sat around the old barn, plunged in deep thought. Henry, the oldest member (aged 12¼) had said in a moment of inspiration:

'Let's think of – sumthin' else to do – sumthin' quite fresh from what we've ever done before.'

And the Outlaws were thinking.

They had engaged in mortal combat with one another, they had cooked strange ingredients over a smoking and reluctant flame with a fine disregard of culinary conventions, they had tracked each other over the country-side with gait and complexions intended to represent those of the aborigines of South America, they had even turned their attention to kidnapping (without any striking success), and these occupations had palled.

In all its activities the Society of Outlaws (comprising four members) aimed at a simple, unostentatious mode of procedure. In their shrinking from the glare of publicity they showed an example of unaffected modesty that many other public societies might profitably emulate. The parents of the members were unaware of the very existence of the society. The ill-timed and tactless interference of parents had nipped in the bud many a cherished plan, and by bitter experience the Outlaws had learnt that secrecy was their only protection.

After Reading

Extract 7

The American handed Leamas another cup of coffee and said, 'Why don't you go back and sleep? We can ring you if he shows up.'

Leamas said nothing, just stared through the window of the checkpoint, along the empty street.

'You can't wait for ever, sir. Maybe he'll come some other time. We can have the polizei contact the Agency: you can be back here in twenty minutes.'

'No,' said Leamas, 'it's nearly dark now.'

'But you can't wait for ever; he's nine hours over schedule.'

'If you want to go, go. You've been very good,' Leamas added. I'll tell Kramer you've been damn good.'

'But how long will you wait?'

'Until he comes.' Leamas walked to the observation window and stood between the two motionless policemen. Their binoculars were trained on the Eastern checkpoint.

'He's waiting for the dark,' Leamas muttered. 'I know he is.'

'This morning you said he'd come across with the workmen.'

Leamas turned on him.

'Agents aren't aeroplanes. They don't have schedules. He's blown, he's on the run, he's frightened. Mundt's after him, now, at this moment. He's only got one chance. Let him choose his time.'

The younger man hesitated, wanting to go and not finding the moment.

A bell rang inside the hut. They waited, suddenly alert. A policeman said in German, 'Black Opel Rekord, Federal registration.'

'He can't see that far in the dusk, he's guessing,' the American whispered and then he added: 'How did Mundt know?'

'Shut up,' said Leamas from the window.

After Reading

Two more novels for comparison

Printed below and on pages 82-83 are two more novels written in 2001, the year before *Spies* was published. Both tell stories of gangs of boys growing up during or soon after the Second World War.

- On your own, read both extracts, then choose one of the extracts to look at in more detail.

- Talk first about your response to the extract in its own right. Did you enjoy it? Would you like to read more? What themes seem to be important? How would you describe the style?

- Go on to explore the extract in relation to *Spies*. You should think about similarities and differences in:
    - the story being told
    - characters
    - themes/issues/motifs
    - relationships
    - the way the story is told (including narrative voice, style, language choices).

- Either as a class, or in groups of four, feed back your ideas about the extract you've studied and what new insights it gives you into the particular qualities of *Spies*.

Five Boys by Mick Jackson

Hector put his mouth up to Bobby's ear.

'You know what?' he whispered. 'If I were you, I'd just start running.'

There was no appeal – no arbitration. For a second Bobby froze. Then he turned and ran – towards the Captain's cottage and the whole unknown world beyond. And as he ran some of the other children hung over the wall and watched, more excited than at any sports day they would ever attend.

Bobby ran for his life and for those few seconds Devon was almost transcended. In his terror he almost managed to shake off the misery that had plagued his every waking hour. The village was obscured. Its sounds fell away, its faces retreated. Then suddenly Bobby felt his feet hit the ground, could hear himself puffing and panting. Could hear the Five Boys start up after him.

He didn't get far before they caught him. He surrendered as if he knew what he was guilty of. The Boys took him by the arms and led him away, like the German pilot in the photograph Bobby had cut out a few days earlier whose plane had been downed in a Wiltshire field. And he was taken round the back of the houses and down a path onto some allotments with their sheds and canes and rows of vegetables.

Barely a word was said throughout the whole proceedings. Bobby was bundled into a hutch and the door was locked behind him with an almost professional manner. The box wasn't much bigger than a coffin and was rich with the ammonial stink of poultry excrement. The Boys stood and watched Bobby kick at the door and tug at the chicken wire and after a while they turned and walked quietly away.

They couldn't have been gone more than a couple of minutes. It was only when Bobby saw them heading back that he made a sound. More words and tears came out of him in those few moments than had come out of him the whole week before. The Boys strode towards him in their gas masks, carrying their pesticide sprayers. They crouched down at the chicken wire and peered

After Reading

in at him. And despite all his kicking and screaming, they pumped some pressure into their sprayers, aimed them in at Bobby and turned them on.

They sprayed him from head to toe. Soaked every twisting inch of him. Pumped long enough to drown a whole army of greenfly. But they found that wearing a gas mask and exerting themselves was altogether different from simply sitting at their desk. And long before they ceased, through sheer exhaustion, and with the thrill of tormenting the evacuee still flooding through their veins, the Boys were already beginning to speculate on the ultimate price of such terrible fun.

Half the posters on the classroom wall warned about germs bringing the nation to its knees. Perhaps they could claim they really *were* fumigating him. 'Germs' and 'Germans' were close enough to be almost indistinguishable and if Bobby wasn't quite German he was about as foreign as they come.

deadkidsongs by Toby Litt

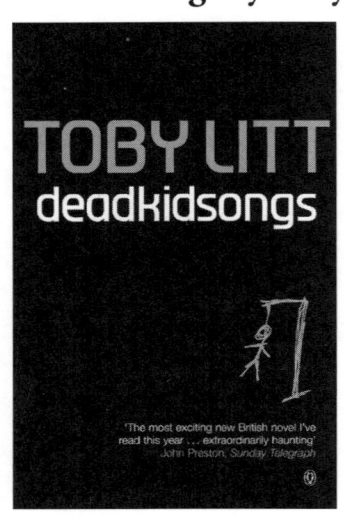

'Fall in!'

It was Andrew's father, calling up from the first-floor landing. (How we honoured him for respecting his son enough to do this!)

We clambered down the narrow staircase, and lined up in front of the Major General (aka Andrew's father).

Sometimes he was the Major-General, and sometimes he was just Andrew's father. It was easy to tell which was which: the two characters had completely different voices.

'And how are the troops today?' he asked. 'Bearing up, I hope. Not just lying rotting in your pits.'

'No, sir,' we barked, together,

We were standing stiffly to attention, as we always did when the Major-General was present.

'At ease, men,' he replied, 'at ease.'

[***]

Andrew started to laugh. Foolishly, we joined in.

'That was far too easy,' shouted the Major-General. 'What in Christ's name were you thinking of?'

Andrew stopped laughing as suddenly as if he'd been pinched, slapped, stabbed, shot.

'You're a disgrace to the entire regiment,' the Major-General said. 'I suppose it's you who were in charge of this mission.'

'Yes, sir, I was,' said Andrew, eyes lowered.

For a moment the Major-General's countenance seemed to brighten, thunderclouds passing. But then, eyes flashing lightning, he reached down, and picked his son up. With ease, he put him over his shoulder. Andrew's head hung down his father's back, his legs kicking uselessly in the air in front of his chest.

We stood up from the nettle patch.

Andrew's father had turned away from us, and was carrying his son down with unmistakeable intent towards The Lake. He had reached the bank before we could catch up. He bent forward, and flipped Andrew, still upside-down, off his back and into his arms. Then, almost cradling him, almost tenderly, began to swing him back and forth. It was both a parody of the earliest days of fatherhood and the ultimate fulfilment of fatherhood's deepest essence: to punish. 'On the count of three,' he shouted. 'One..., Two...'

Of course, we knew what was going to happen. No-one could have been surer of it than Andrew, and than him, no-one could have approved of it more wholeheartedly. Yet we needed, once again, even after so many times, to have our faith in fatherhood reconfirmed. We needed to see that there was Justice, and that Justice would exercise a clemency far beyond the immediate incidence. 'I am being harsh with you now,' this was what Andrew's father's actions all implied. 'Because the world will be far harsher with you, later. You must be prepared for this harshness, so that you may be able properly to withstand it.'

We saw Andrew's blond hair, so like our own, swaying, his arms dangling. We heard his screams of futile resistance.

'Three,' shouted the Major-General, his father, and threw him far out above the dark-glassy surface of The Lake.

[**]

It very quickly became clear to us that Andrew was going to be all right. The paleness of his skin and the weakness of his cough, these might have suggested an imminent departure. But we continued to feel his presence within us. And, after a couple of minutes, lying on the path by the side of The Lake, Andrew opened his eyes. During all this time, the Best Father had knelt touchingly by his side. 'Come on, lad,' he'd said, 'snap out of it.' He'd also said, 'Stop larking around.' And once, just once, he'd whispered, 'Kangeroo.' This, we knew, was an almost prehistoric nickname for our friend, our leader. It dated all the way back to when Andrew couldn't properly pronounce his own name. Andrew's father hadn't called his own son Kangeroo in years. We knew what it meant. We saw how terribly much he loved him. So much so that, for almost all of the time, he denied himself the greatest joy, the joy of expressing his love.

[**]

Andrew recovered enough first to sit and then to stand up.

'You're all right now, aren't you?' said the Best Father.

'I'm fine,' Andrew replied, bending over to breathe, the palms of his hands braced against his kneecaps.

'Very rash of you to jump in like that,' said the Best Father. It was in ways like this that Andrew's father almost managed to be one of us. Unlike most grown-ups, he recognized the absolute necessity of coming up with a lie every time something happened about which one might be questioned. This was to be our lie, Gang lie, for all other grown-ups, for all others full-stop. If asked, we would say Andrew had rashly jumped into The Lake. There was no need for the Best Father to add, 'And especially don't tell your mother what really happened.' Mothers, it was obvious, must never, on any account, be told what had really happened. This we had learned from the Best Father. Mothers simply could not handle the truth of things. Yet our devotion to the lie went far beyond the immediate: this lie, like all our lies, was to be universal.

Critical Responses

The digested read

The Saturday *Guardian* includes a series in which they summarise a recently published novel in no more than 400 words. Although it is a light-hearted column claiming to save their readers the bother of actually reading the novel, the digested reads strive not only to capture the essential points of the story, but to do so 'in the style of the original'.

- In pairs, make notes on what you would include in a digested read of *Spies.*
- Share your ideas as a class and talk about how you would reflect the style of the novel in your digested read.
- On your own have a go at writing a digested read for *Spies.*
- In groups of four, take it in turns to read out your digested reads and talk about what each person has foregrounded/marginalised in terms of content and style.
- Now read the *Guardian* version on page 85 and compare it with your own and those of other people in the class.

As you've seen, the *Guardian* also publishes a one line summary 'the digested read, digested'.

- On your own write a sentence of no more than 20 words, summing up what you think is essential in the novel.
- Take it in turns to read these aloud and talk about the similarities and differences in your interpretations of what *Spies* is about.

The critics

Reading the critics

Included on pages 86-88 is a selection of extracts from reviews of *Spies.*

- Read all the review extracts through once, ticking anything you agree with and crossing anything you disagree with.
- Use an A3 photocopy of the chart on page 89 to focus your exploration of the critics' responses. If possible, work in groups of four, sharing the extracts between you, then feeding back your analysis.
- Talk about the approach each reviewer takes in writing about the novel. To what extent is the critic describing, analysing or evaluating the novel?

Using the critics

The following activities all use the reviews to help you develop your own, independent interpretation of the novel.

- Share out the longer reviews (numbers 15-17 on page 88) and, for the one you have been allocated, analyse in more detail what it is that the reviewer is focusing attention on (for example, themes, character, language, structure, personal response).
- Use the review extract as the starting point for an essay or a lecture.
- Continue the review.
- Write a letter to the literary editor of the newspaper, exploring in detail why you agree or disagree with what the reviewer is saying.
- Use it as the starting point for a 'just a minute' response to the novel.

Critical Responses

Spies by Michael Frayn
Condensed in the style of the original

There it is again, the same sweet smell of privet. Now all kinds of things come back to me. Everything is as it was, yet everything is changed. It is 50 years since I was last here at the Close. There are the Averys and there is Trewinnick, home to the Juice. And is that Stephen Wheatley playing with his friend Keith?

I was always aware of my fortune in having Keith as my friend. We wore the same S-belts to school, but his are the colours of the local preparatory school while mine are for the wrong school. I am the other ranks to his officer class.

It was Keith who found the crashed German aircraft and the apeman running amok on the golf course. And it was Keith who changed everything when he announced that his mother was a German spy. How do I feel? Envious that it is not my mother, and yet privileged that he confided in me. The Haywards had nothing to do with any other families in the Close, apart from Keith's Aunty Dee and Uncle Pete, who was away serving in the RAF.

As we began to follow her movements, it began to make sense that she should be a spy. Did I not detect falsity when she poured the lemon barley water? And when we searched her diary what were those mysterious monthly x's?

We retired to our hideout in the bushes to keep watch. We watched her go to Aunty Dee's and disappear several times. This wasn't a ghost story, but something infinitely more frightening. She was going through the narrow tunnel under the railway into the dense woodland.

Keith and I found the padlocked tin with 20 Craven A inside, and spied his mother entering a disused underground cellar. We heard an old tramp's cough as we banged on the roof.

'Was that you Stephen?' she said sadly later. 'I warned you that some things were best kept secret.'

I wasn't invited to Keith's much after that, but one evening his mother asked me to take some things to the cellar. There were noises. It was me they were after, but they got the old tramp. The train sliced him in half. It was my fault.

Keith was right, though. There was a German spy. It was me; we had emigrated to Britain in 1935 and it was to Germany I returned after the war. And did I know it wasn't an old tramp, but Uncle Pete instead? Of course I did, but even after I heard him speak I still imagined him to be a German. It is time to go now; thank you for having me.

And if you really are pressed: The digested read, digested...
A Proustian whiff of privet brings back disturbing wartime childhood secrets.

Critical Responses

1. *Spies* is a novel in which different layers of irony are nested like Russian dolls. *London Review of Books*

2. I was reminded of L.P. Hartley's *The Go-Between*. That made a memorable film, and *Spies* would too. Just as Hartley evoked the tensions underneath the spreading cedars on the eve of the First World War, so *Spies* delineates the cracks behind the privet hedge during the Second. *The Mail on Sunday*

3. *Spies* explores the order we impose on the ambiguous chaos of reality, and the almost universal tendency to paranoia involved in trying to make sense of the world [...] Frayn's ingenious treatment of perception gains moral weight when it comes to be about identity, and the kind of double think that people half know is untrue. Phil Baker, *The Daily Telegraph*

4. What carries the day is the sense of adult drama off-stage, the carefully chosen period detail. Hugo Barnacle, *New Statesman*

5. It is a study of what we think we know and what is real, and also of the difference between what we really know and what we are prepared to admit. It is a dark book and a sad one. John Lanchester, *The New York Review of Books*

6. [...] begins in friendship and spirals out into a galaxy of questions of loyalty, guilt and complicity, the unknowability of others and the strange dark matter at the fringes of the self. Jennifer Schuessler, *The New York Times Book Review*

7. This is such a sensuous book that at times, while never trying to be poetic or melodic, it comes near to painting or music [...] The distinction of this novel is in evocation of lost landscape [...] As always Frayn has made a usual subject entirely his own. Jane Gardam, *The Spectator*

8. It is an odd, original haunting little tale in which the teller is the really interesting thing [...] But the book's real merit lies in the way Stephen comes to understand the truth behind the mysteries of his world by beginning to understand something about the difference between men and women. This is achieved entirely without crudity [...] A modest but entirely memorable book. Robert Nye, *The Times*

9. *Spies* draws much of its force from the narrative's subtly inverted echoes of other novels. Jonathan Keates, *TLS*

Critical Responses

10 Michael Frayn's playful *Spies* is an alarming, dizzying whirligig of deception [...] he examines a crisis of conscience in a triple treat of a novel [...] It is equal parts compelling war story, painful love story and unravelling mystery [...] Frayn holds back the biggest secret of *Spies* until the closing chapter. A surprise revelation comes as something of a jolt. It's a bit of a trick, but Frayn manages to pull off the final gamble in this delicately balanced deciphering of the surreptitious codes of childhood. Robert Allen Papinchak, Special for *USA Today*

11 The book is deftly plotted, with the elderly Stephen commingling naturally with his younger self. [...] *Spies* is as much a work of suspense as it is of saddened reflection. Frayn is a master of the casual surprise, and the surprises here all ring true [...] The tone is anguished and humorous by turns. It could be argued that there are too many revelations in the final pages, but otherwise this is a deeply satisfying account of the everyday torments and confusions experienced by a not especially bright boy at a time of international madness. Frayn has written nothing better. Paul Bailey, *The Independent*

12 Critics are equally lavish in their praise of *Spies*, considered by many to be Frayn's finest novel. The story begins simply with an adventure devised by Keith and Stephen, two schoolboys growing up in World War II. When Keith decides that his mother is a German spy, the children mount a spying campaign that propels them into an adult world of intrigue, secrecy, fear and heartbreak. The plot is slick and tense, but Frayn's real triumph is to portray the tangled dreams and perceptions of childhood as if Stephen's world was his own domain. *Daily Mail* interview for *Daily Mail Book Club*

13 Throughout this book Frayn writes as if he must close each act with a zinger to keep you in your seat while the curtain is down. We have a lot of 'Everything has changed once again, and changed forever.'

The unnecessary and empty suspense can't jibe with Frayn's insistence that the book be cast as a recollection. The same is true for the wilful naïveté of the child narrator. If we are not to benefit from the older man's perspective until the last dozen or so pages, why introduce him at the start? Max Watman, *New Criterion*

14 The setting has something of *The Go-Between*, *Whistle Down the Wind* or *Just William* in the ironic discrepancy between the childish and adult worlds – with a bit of Golding's *Lord of the Flies* thrown into the mix for good measure. Toby Litt's *deadkidsongs* was a sulphuric treatment of the same let's-pretend theme.

This is a lovingly conceived, handsomely detailed novel in a conservative vein with a vivid sympathy for how lonely, scared and helpless being a child feels, and how eagerly we forget it. It is about memory and imagination.

The plot is like an aircraft [...] that spends a puzzlingly long time taxiing along the runway before it finally gets airborne. Even then, it is only in the final 50 pages that Frayn pulls back the joystick, and with a great whoosh we are up for some very showy loop the loops and victory rolls [...] *Spies* is not as sophisticated or ambitious as Frayn's last novel, *Headlong,* but it is never less than witty, ingenious and a pleasure to read. Peter Bradshaw, *The Guardian*

Critical Responses

His latest novel, *Spies*, is very different from the erudition of *Copenhagen* or *Headlong*. It is a slim piquant novel of childhood, set during the Second World War, in which a small boy becomes ensnared in adult deceptions after a game of spying gets out of hand. Stephen is an impressionable child whose make-believe world becomes poisoned by the suggestion, made by his best friend, that his friend's mother is a spy [...] While *Spies* would seem to be more personal than his previous novels, Frayn insists it is just as painstakingly researched: 'It is just that the research I did was trying to remember what it felt like.' This research project is embodied in the novel by the older Stephen, who revisits his childhood home to try to grope his way to an understanding of what went on in the head of the 'monochrome' child he was all those years ago. It's one of the unsettling features of the novel that you're never quite sure how much is felt and how much is informed reconstruction [...] in *Spies* it takes the reader to the point in childhood at which memory is formed, before there are any reference points to give those memories a context or a perspective. As the philosopher in him says: 'It's not what has happened that makes the next thing happen, it's how people perceive what has happened.'
The Guardian, Jan 31st, 2002

The sheer foreignness of childhood requires that he use the third person as often as the first ... Physical sensations – the feel of a tumbler of lemon barley, the taste of chocolate spread – survive better in the mind than past states of mind. This can seem a rather perverse piece of construction, setting up a double perspective and then muffling it, but its great virtue is it shuts out whimsy. [...] The key to the book's success is Frayn's decision to respect young Stephen's point of view without staking everything on recreating it [...] *Spies* works as a mystery, as a war story and as a coming-of-age narrative. The only thing it can't quite be, despite its author's intellectual background, is a work of philosophy. There are some slightly strained passages, ponderings with a whiff of the seminar, rather too methodical for the context. [...] Adults and children, males and females, make different accommodations with their own knowings and unknowings. Girls in particular (nice touch in a reconfigured boys' adventure story) seem to have an early mental puberty. They grasp truths immediately, leaving boys lamely deducing in their wake. Adam Mars-Jones, *The Observer*

Fictional evocations of children tragically misapprehending adult realities are two-a-penny. This is the plot of *Spies*; but one transfigured by Michael Frayn's crackling intelligence. The novel, indeed, is almost disconcertingly tightly constructed. It contains social comedy, humanity, black tragi-comedy and tragedy – but all held quite deliberately at arms length, within the retrospective framework of a pensioner's reconstruction of his wartime childhood. [...] For, of course, there is a real, adult secret, or secrets. I guessed the outlines of the truth less than half way through; but this only made the rest of the novel horribly full of extra tension. For its tragedy as well as its comedy are intrinsically and almost cruelly shaped by our superior knowledge – rather like a theatrical audience knowing more than Othello – so that even, or indeed especially, if you solve the 'mystery', you will still be on tenterhooks to discover what damage their ignorance will cause [...] All the rest of *Spies* actually improves upon re-reading, which is the true test of depth. It is cerebral and sensuous; extremely funny and yet deeply serious about the peculiar mixture of curiosity and profound incuriousness that characterises children – and, Frayn suggests, adults too. Caroline Moore, *The Sunday Telegraph*

Critical Responses

Review	Main focus of review	Reviewer's approach (e.g. analytical, descriptive, evaluative)	Agree/disagree and why
1			
2			
3			
4			
5			
6			
7			
8			
9			
10			
11			
12			
13			
14			
15			
16			
17			

Critical Responses

Writing a book club guide

Spies is a popular choice for book clubs and reading groups. In December 2004 it was the *Daily Mail's* book club choice with many readers posting their responses to the novel on the message board.

- Talk about why you think it is a popular choice for book clubs.

- In pairs, or small groups, devise and write a guide for a reading group. Some of the things you could include are listed here.
    - A synopsis
    - Questions to focus discussion
    - Reviews
    - Interview extracts
    - Suggestions for further reading

You can see examples of reading guides for a wide range of fiction and non-fiction books at the following websites:

- http://www.randomhouse.co.uk/readersgroup/readingguides.htm
- http://www.booksattransworld.co.uk/feet/readingguides.htm
- http://www.readinggroupguides.com/findaguide/index.asp
- http://www.harpercollins.com/readers.asp

Teachers' Notes

A map of the locations

You might find the following notes useful in working out the locations of the story. Pages 9, 11, 23, 29, 32 and 37 of the novel are particularly helpful.

Here's a checklist of the main places that should feature on the maps:
- The train station
- The main road
- The small parade of shops
- The Avenue
- The Close
- The postbox
- The railway tunnel
- The railway line
- The Barns
- The Cottages
- The Lanes

In the Close there should be 14 houses:
- The Sheldons
- The Geest twins (No. 5)
- Wentworth (No. 2 where Stephen lived)
- The Pinchers (No. 3)
- Lamorna (No 6, Barbara Berrill, Deirdre and their mother)
- Chollerton (the Haywards No. 9)
- Trewinnick (the 'Juice')
- The lookout (No. 4 Braemar, now Meadowhurst, Miss Durrant's bombed out house)
- Auntie Dee's house (3 doors down on the same side of the street, almost opposite Stephen's)
- The Hardiments at No. 1
- The Stotts (Norman and Eddie) at No. 10 or No. 13
- The Averys (Charlie and Dave) or the McAfees at No. 7
- One of the Averys, McAfees and Stotts at No. 10 or 13
- Mr. Gort, No. 12

The map on page 92 is one attempt to create a visual representation of the settings. It may not be flawless but could be helpful for students to compare with their own.

Teachers' Notes

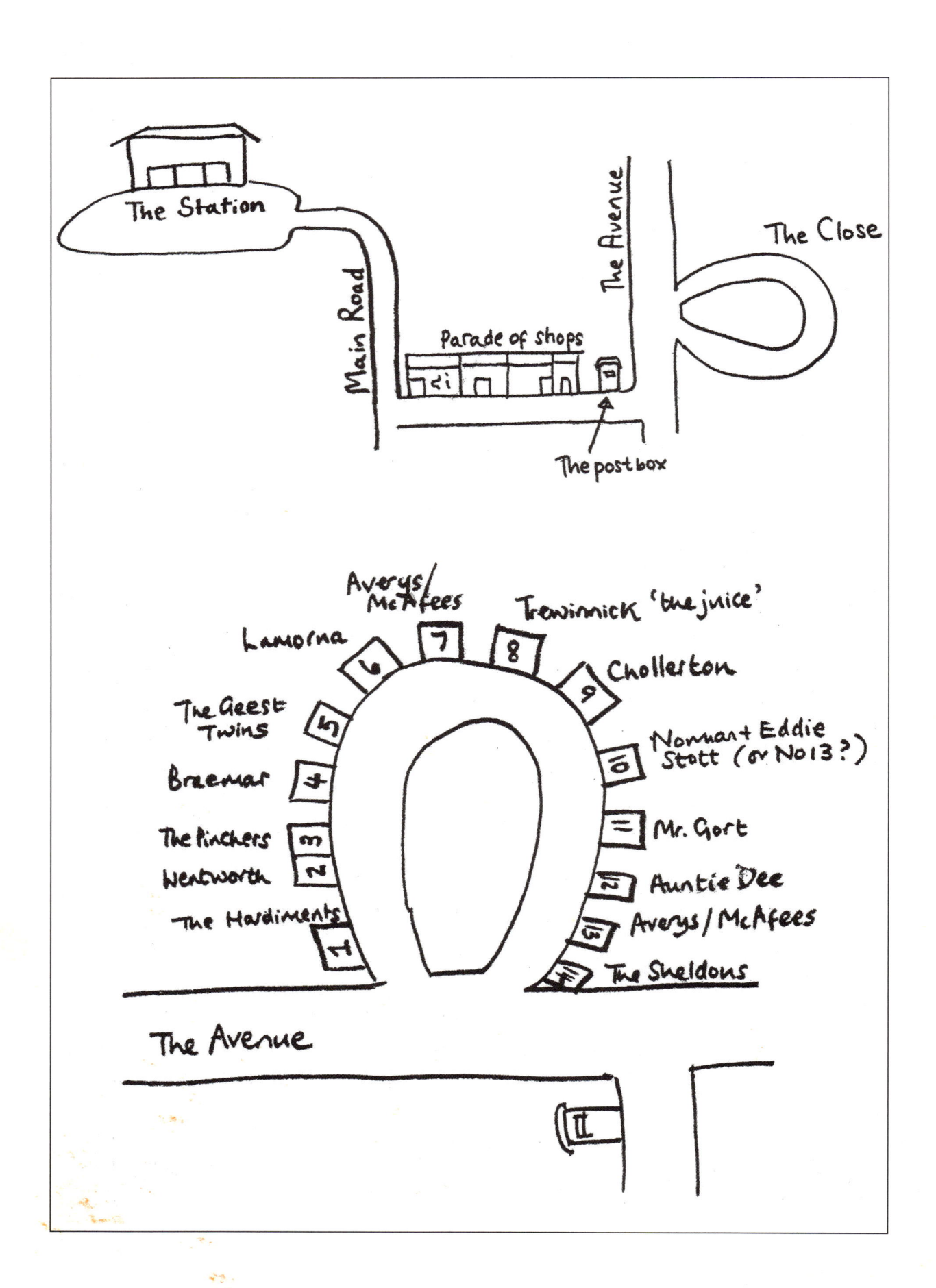

92 — Studying *Spies* — © English and Media Centre, 2005

Teachers' Notes

What happens in Chapter 10

You might find the following summary of what happens in Chapter 10 useful when working on '"The game's finally over." What's happened?' on page 48. NB: this is not a definitive account, just our interpretation developed in conjunction with teachers attending the English and Media Centre course on *Spies*.

- Mrs Hayward asks Stephen to take the basket of food to the man in the Barns.

- Barbara and Stephen look in the basket.

- Mr Hayward confiscates the basket.

- Stephen realises the man will be waiting for the food he should have been brought and decides he will have to take him something.

- Stephen takes his family's emergency rations from the cupboard under the stairs.

- The man names him 'Stephen'.

- The man gives Stephen what Stephen thinks is a silk scarf and a message ('for ever') to take to Mrs Hayward.

- Keith bullies Stephen, cutting his neck with the 'bayonet'.

- Stephen tries, but fails, to keep this from his parents and Geoff. He cries and doesn't say anything.

- His parents say they will get the police in the morning.

- That night in bed Stephen realises the policeman will find the scarf he has been unable to give to Mrs Hayward and that this will betray both her and the man.

- He decides he must hide it and realises the only possible place for it is in the tunnel.

- He goes out into the night and hears/sees a number of men with cars and flashlights.

- They are obviously searching for someone. (At no point is it made clear to Stephen or the reader whether they are searching for Uncle Peter – the deserter – or the 'tramp'/'sexual deviant'. Nor do we ever know why they have come looking on this night in this place; whether, for example, someone has tipped them off – mothers worried about the 'sexual deviant', or Mr Hayward, possibly. If the latter, does he know the man is Uncle Peter?)

- Stephen first assumes he has led the men to the man in the Barns, then changes his mind and thinks they have come for him.

- In the tunnel he sees a train carrying bits of a British bomber plane as its cargo. (This bit of the narrative is particularly elliptical.)

- The men get what they were looking for: 'Got him?'; 'Most of him,'.

- (The adult?) Stephen reflects that the man must have tried to run away from the men chasing him, missed his footing, fallen onto the railway line, been electrocuted and cut up by the train.

The general air of Chapter 10 is surreal – the child's confused perception (at night, he already feels guilty, is not admitting to himself what he knows and his involvement in what has been going on); the older narrator is reliving the night with no more factual knowledge, only an adult's interpretation of his earlier experience. Chapter 11 does include some filling in of the gaps, for example the scarf is actually part of a map that all airmen had to help them find their way if brought down in Germany.

© English and Media Centre, 2005   Studying *Spies*

Teachers' Notes

A focus on language – a close reading activity on an extract

The following approach works well for any passage you want to focus on in detail. You could for example use it as an alternative to, or an extension of the activity on pages 38-41. Pairs or groups of students are asked to analyse the passage, focusing on just one aspect of its language. They then report back to the whole class. Possible aspects to focus on are suggested here. You might decide to narrow the scope of the analysis by focusing on only two or three of these aspects.

1. Lexis
2. Tense
3. Sentence length and structure
4. Images, symbols and motifs
5. Narrative voice
6. Sound effects
7. Paragraphing
8. Narrative structure
9. Repetition
10. Parallels and oppositions

On page 95 are notes on the opening of one of the extracts (re-printed below), showing some of the features that students might notice under each of the headings. It is not exhaustive but gives an indication of the sort of comments you might encourage students to make. Students need to go on to explore in more detail the effect of the features they observe.

Passage 1

I should go through the darkness of the tunnel. On my own. And out into the moonlight beyond.

If only I had a knotted rope...

The white stillness goes on and on. I've never seen the world like this before.

Slowly it comes to me that I don't actually need a knotted rope. I could simply walk down the stairs.

Now I've thought the thought, I know I have to do it. I know I'm going to do it.

And at once I'm terrified. The summer night has become suddenly freezing. I start to shiver so uncontrollably that I can scarcely get the jumper over my head or the sandals on my feet. I can hear my teeth rattling together like dice in a shaker. Geoff stirs in his sleep, as if he'd heard them too. I feel my way downstairs, and through the kitchen to the back door. Very slowly I ease back the bolt, still shaking. I step silently out into the silver darkness, and become part of it.

Never in my life before have I crept out of the house in the middle of the night. Never before have I experienced this great stillness, or this strange new freedom to go anywhere and do anything.

I shan't have the courage to go through with it, of course. I shall die of fear before I get beyond the end of the street.

I must do it, though, I must.

****

Between the reflected disc of silver-grey behind me and the second one in front of me is a darkness whose shape is defined entirely by sound. The huge reverberations of the water plopping from the wet blackness overhead into the black water beside me merge into suites of scutterings and splashings trailed by unseen nocturnal creatures fleeing before the long echoes of my panicky breathing. In my terror I lose my footing on the unseen narrow causeway along the edge of the unseen lake, and have to keep touching the slime on the walls to steady myself. The slime is full of germs – I'm getting germs all over my hands.

Teachers' Notes

1. Lexis
- Simple, monosyllabic, Anglo-Saxon words at the start, reflecting the child's immediate experience
- Shift in 2nd section to a more adult way of telling, reflected in more latinate, polysyllabic vocabulary

2. Tense
- Present tense – sense of immediacy
- Future tense, suggesting his fears for the future

3. Sentence length and structure
- Minor sentences, like 'On my own.' and 'And into the moonlight beyond.' suggestive of his thoughts
- Simple and compound sentences rather than complex sentences in the first part

4. Images, symbols and motifs
- Moonlight – connotations of thrillers, or perhaps frightening fairy tales
- Images taken from a child's world: 'teeth like dice in a shaker'
- 'germs' – a motif in the book as a whole

5. Narrative voice
- Reconstruction of a child's voice, with some of its qualities (e.g. 'and' as a connective) but also adult vocabulary and reflection, particularly in the second part

6. Sound effects
- 's' sounds in first part suggest whispering and secrecy. Later onomatopoeia used to convey noise, as a contrast with moments of silence: 'ploppings', 'scutterings', 'splashing'

7. Paragraphing
- Disjointed one or two sentence paragraphs – suggest the boy's movements, sense of terror; later, when he's out of the house, longer descriptive paragraph

8. Narrative structure
- 1st section persuading himself to do it
- Then the doing of it – out in the night

9. Repetition
- Sentence structure – 'Never...Never'; 'I must...I must'
- 'germs', 'breathing'

10. Parallels and oppositions
- Sound/silence
- Stillness/movement
- Inside/outside
- Fear/courage
- Darkness/moonlight
- Breathing/not breathing
- Thinking/doing

© English and Media Centre, 2005 Studying *Spies*

Teachers' Notes

An example of segmenting the novel

Here is one way in which the novel could be divided into sections for the activities on pages 66-68.

- The memory (Ch 1 and 2 to 'Close shifts in front of my eyes.')
- The Close (to the end of Ch 2)
- Spying (first part Ch 3)
- Keith (second part Ch 3)
- Disappearing act (Ch 4)
- An old man (opening Ch 5)
- Revelation (main section Ch 5)
- Privet (end Ch 5)
- The tunnel (first part Ch 6)
- The Lanes (second part Ch 6)
- Everything has changed; everything is the same (first part Ch 7)
- Complicity (main part Ch 7)
- Time passing (opening Ch 8)
- Sex (Ch 8)
- The basket (first part Ch 9)
- Into the darkness (end part Ch 9)
- The message (first part Ch 10)
- The end of the game (second part Ch 10)
- Finally over (end Ch 10)
- Heimweh and Fernweh (Ch 11)

Genre

The extracts on pages 76-80 are taken from the following novels.

1. Clare George: *The Cloud Chamber* (2001)

2. L.P. Hartley: *The Go-Between* (1953)

3. Enid Blyton: *Five Go Off to Camp* (1948)

4. Richard Bucchan: *The Thirty-Nine Steps* (1915)

5. Marcel Proust: *Swann's Way* (1913)

6. Richmal Crompton: *Just William* (1922)

7. Le Carré: *The Spy Who Came in From the Cold* (1963)